Christian Issues
in Southern Asia

by **P. D. DEVANANDAN**

Christian Issues in Southern Asia

Friendship Press **NEW YORK**

LIBRARY OF CONGRESS CATALOG CARD NUMBER: 63–8682

COPYRIGHT © 1963 BY FRIENDSHIP PRESS, INC.
Printed in the United States of America

Contents

5

CONTENTS

CONTENTS

7

CONTENTS

Preface

Christian Issues in Southern Asia comes to its readers without the final guiding hand of its author. Dr. Devanandan died August 10, 1962, before he could make contemplated changes and additions in the first draft of his manuscript. He had wanted particularly to enlarge his treatment of Buddhism and Islam in terms of their contemporary renascence, but his plans for such a section were never realized.

Dr. Devanandan's book, however, is in no way an incomplete or unfinished work. It is rather the natural and complete summation of a lifetime's study of the relevancy of the Christian faith in Southern Asia. As such, it demonstrates the author's concern for Christian unity as a means of strengthening the witness of the church and his desire that members of the "older" churches accept new Christians as their brothers in Christ.

If this book, the author's last testimony to his faith, can stir the reader to new insights and renewed commitment to the mission of the church in the world, it will serve as a continuing memorial to the man who taught that the Christian faith is a "true fellowship with God and with one another."

CHAPTER *1*

The Background of History

THIS survey of Southern Asia includes the four different countries of India, Pakistan, Ceylon, and Nepal. They are close neighbors, although in land stretch and population strength they vary widely from one another. People in these four countries speak different languages. In fact, within each country, there is literally a babel of tongues. Different religions also mark the region. Hindus, Muslims, Buddhists, and a small minority of Christians are found everywhere in varying proportions. The past history of these lands records a good deal of cultural interpenetration, and at present there is evidence of many common problems.

NEPAL

Nepal was almost unknown to the West for centuries. But in the past decade it has been thrust into the foreground of the international scene. This is largely due to its strategic position between India and Chinese-occupied Tibet. Only since 1950 have the social and political forces of the modern world made their impact on the Nepalese. What was once a medieval kingdom now is being transformed almost overnight into a modern nation-state. Of course, Nepal's history goes back to ancient times, for, from the very early days of Buddhism, the kingdom was known as a seat of Buddhist culture.

Though the Nepalese always have been nominally self-governing, for most of their history they have been either directly or indirectly under some measure of foreign domination. Nepal was an early tributary of China, while Indian authority was particularly strong during the great empires of Samudragupta (335–376) and of Sri Harsha (604–647). In 1815 Nepal, almost in its present geographical extent, came under British influence. In 1947 relations between Nepal and independent India were established as between two sovereign states. After a period of political unrest, due to the transformation by local leadership of a feudal government into a constitutional monarchy, Nepal seems to be settling down somewhat.

The population is a little more than nine million. This makes for an average of about 170 persons per square mile, which is more than three times the average for the United States.

Nepal is a nation of more or less self-sufficient villages whose societies are largely organized on a tribal basis, especially in the hill areas. The tribal folk describe themselves as either Hindus or Buddhists. However, closer observation of their religious beliefs and practices shows that no sharp line can be drawn between the Hindu and the Buddhist groups. In many places the two faiths have become so fused that the gods and shrines of popular worship seem to be the same.

The more numerous Hindus are mostly worshipers of the popular god, Siva. This is the religion of the ruling class as well as that of the powerful tribe of Gurkhas.

Nepalese Buddhism is of the Mahayana school, which does not adhere to the teachings of Buddha in regard to God and the hereafter. Buddha taught that belief in God and gods was irrelevant. Man could find release from the law of karma, the consequences of his own actions, only by determined effort. When he did find release it was in nirvana, total annihilation. Mahayana

Buddhism, however, accepts belief in gods. Through worshiping them, man is held able to gain supernatural help in his effort to find release. Also the final goal of nirvana is not to be regarded as a negative state of nothingness but as a positive state of supreme bliss. Obviously these beliefs have been influenced by Hinduism, which is willing to accept Buddha himself as a deity among other deities. Nepalese Buddhists in turn have come to regard Hindu deities as objects of worship.

Besides the classical gods and goddesses of the Hindu pantheon, popular religion in Nepal finds a place for the worship of various mountain gods. These cults are only of local importance, but they play a very significant role in the life of the people. There is also a small Muslim population in Nepal, most of whom are traders who have come from India.

Christians are very rare. As early as 1768, Nepal refused permission for Christian missionaries to enter the country for direct evangelistic work. Since 1951 this policy has been relaxed, permission now being given to missionaries who agree to severely confine their activities to social service, education, and medical work.

Modern Nepal is profoundly concerned about education and public health. No exact figures are available on the rate of illiteracy, but the general opinion is that it ranges from 91 to 98 per cent of the population. There is yet no common language spoken by all the Nepalese

document language
Nepali become

and this is a serious handicap. But Nepali (of Hindi derivation) is spoken as a second language by many people and seems to be gradually replacing the tribal languages in some areas. A national education planning commission, set up by the government in 1953, has worked out ambitious plans. The goals suggested are voluntary universal primary education by 1975 and compulsory universal primary education by 1985. At the same time, it may be noted that the commission's estimate was that only 3.5 per cent of Nepalese school-age children are enrolled in the 1,320 schools. Universal literacy is second in importance to primary education in the commission's recommendations. The program calls for literacy classes for one hundred thousand adults per year by 1965. To be fully realized, this program will probably need outside financial assistance as well as the guidance of skilled literacy workers.

Ninety-nine per cent of the population of Nepal, *No medical care* according to one recent estimate, is without adequate medical care. Malaria is rampant everywhere, and so also is tuberculosis. The Nepalese have little resistance to these diseases because of insufficient and ill-balanced diets. But improvement of public health in Nepal, as in many other Asian lands, must be a process of improving economic conditions, changing social institutions, improving general hygienic conditions, and altering popular habits.

CEYLON

The island of Ceylon has much in common with India. This is no doubt due to the close historical association between the two countries over the centuries. Racially the Ceylonese are probably of the same Aryan and Dravidian stock as the people in North and South India. Indian influence accounts for the presence of both Buddhism and Hinduism, which are the major religions in this island. One tradition holds that a relative of Buddha himself carried the sacred teachings to Ceylon, and Buddhism is today the popular faith of the Sinhalese who live mostly in the southern part of the country. The Sinhalese (Sanscrit for Ceylonese) form nearly 75 per cent of the population. In the northern part of the island the popular religion is Hinduism, and the people there are Tamils who originally came from South India. They represent some 11 per cent of the population.

In the sixteenth century Ceylon came under Western influence; first Portuguese, then Dutch, and finally British. Great Britain took official possession of the island in 1802, securing her control at a somewhat later date. She ruled until 1948 when Ceylon became an independent member of the British Commonwealth of Nations.

Something more than 8 per cent of the population is

Christian. During the Portuguese occupation many Ceylonese became Catholics "in fear as well as in faith," and even today the Roman Catholic Church is very strong and influential. With the Dutch came Protestantism, which was fiercely intolerant both of the Catholics and of the non-Christians. The British pursued a policy of religious tolerance, but in regard to educational institutions they were undoubtedly of much help to Christian missions.

Since Ceylon became independent, there has been a growing self-awareness among the Buddhists. In 1947 religious relics, formerly taken from India to Great Britain, were returned to Sanchi after a triumphal procession through Buddhist countries. And in 1957 the 2500th anniversary of the Buddha's death was observed with great enthusiasm. A new impetus has been given to translations into Sinhalese of the Buddhist sacred books, the compilation of a Buddhist encyclopedia, and the restoration of Buddhist sacred monuments.

The Buddhists in Ceylon belong to the Theravāda school. This branch of Buddhism claims a special orthodoxy in that it sticks closely to the teachings of the Buddha. The Buddha, meaning the "Enlightened" or the "Awakened," taught that all life is suffering; that there is nothing abiding or permanent, because everything is forever changing; and that there is no such thing as soul, the ultimately real. The one supreme law is the law of karma.[1] According to this law, a person passes through endless lives, each successive one being better or worse according to the good or the evil he has done. The Buddha taught that this cycle could be broken by the law of right living that he set forth.

In order to discipline one's ways strictly according to the Buddhist ethic, it is best to become a *bhikku*, or monk. The Buddhist layman, however, does not seek to reach this same perfection. His family obligations, professional claims, and worldly contacts impose serious limitations on such an attainment. Remembering that the world is sorrowful, transient, and soulless, he tries to eliminate pleasure in everything; to reduce his attachment to worldly things; to moderate his desires; to be satisfied with what he has; and to be diligent in his efforts to attain salvation.

The Buddhist layman is also required to observe the five precepts. These are abstention from: (1) killing any living being; (2) stealing other people's possessions; (3) improper or excessive sexuality; (4) arguments and disputations; and (5) intoxicants. Sometimes Buddhist laymen take a vow to observe these rules more closely during a prescribed period of some days or weeks.

In the Buddhist tradition the ruler of the state upheld the doctrine and was himself supposed to be a model of

[1] Derived from Hindu teachings, *q.v.* p. 75. Karma is the effect of any action on the doer.

Buddhist piety. But during the period of foreign rule in Ceylon this did not obtain. Since independence, the trend has been to restore the old order and recover the Buddhist heritage of the Sinhalese. The first step was to replace English by Sinhalese as the state language. Along with this intention, the entire system of education was scheduled to be remodeled, because English education was believed to lead to denationalization and secularism. Moreover, education in Ceylon had been considerably influenced by Christians. On the eve of independence it was estimated that 35 per cent of all state-aided schools were run by Christians and they managed some 70 per cent of the English-language schools.

The Buddhist revival in Ceylon is in fact a complex phenomenon. It began undoubtedly with the desire to restore Buddhism to its rightful place in the affairs of the country. But this could not be done by simply reverting to the past. The values of the new world of industrial advancement, scientific knowledge, and democratic institutions had to be retained. More than all, national unity had to be preserved. The philosophy and ethic of Theravāda Buddhism, therefore, had to be restated to take contemporary realities into account. In this effort both Buddhist laymen and monks co-operated.

As indicated earlier, there is a powerful minority of Tamils in Ceylon who have a different religious and cultural background. The Hindu Tamils are highly educated and occupy influential places in business, the professions, and government. They resent the imposition of Sinhalese as the national language because they fear that it is a means of relegating them to permanent minority status. Ugly incidents of violence have resulted in some parts of Ceylon in consequence, and some Tamil leaders have been agitating for partition. In 1958 Ceylon experienced horrifying communal riots, never before seen on the island, and in 1961 a state of emergency was declared in the Tamil provinces. It almost seems as if national disunity, not unity, were growing.

The population of Ceylon is rising rapidly. Excepting Taiwan, Ceylon has the highest birth rate in Asian lands today. When the British took over in 1815 the population was approximately one million. Today it is well over nine million and nearly twice what it was before 1946. In the past the economy of the island expanded rapidly enough to give the growing population sufficient employment and a rising standard of living. But now the plantations of rubber, tea, and coconut cannot be expected to yield much more, while the demands and expectations of the Ceylonese people are rapidly increasing.

Industrial development has been very limited, and the extensive national welfare schemes the government has undertaken have proved expensive. Ceylonese leaders are therefore redoubling their efforts to diversify the economy, raise productivity, open new opportunities to the educated, and free the country from its very heavy dependence on the three crops whose future on the world market is uncertain.

The most pressing need of Ceylon is to secure political stability. Party strife within the government and the growing rift between the Sinhalese majority and the Tamil minority, intensified by economic rivalry, religious antagonism, and cultural conflict, have created an altogether unhappy state of affairs. Fortunately, Ceylonese leaders and the people at large are fully aware of the tragic situation, and efforts are being made to set things right through mutual consultation and constitutional reform.

INDIA AND PAKISTAN

Ceylon need politi stabil [handwritten margin note]

Partitioned in 1947 [handwritten margin note]

India and Pakistan can be considered together, for until the partition in 1947 the historical background of these two countries was the same and can be traced back some five thousand years. Even before the Aryans came, there was a fairly advanced culture in the Indus Valley. Archeological discoveries in the Valley reveal that there were well-planned cities in which lived people who even in those days worshiped Siva and practiced yoga, or mental discipline. The Aryans came about 1500 B.C. and drove the "dark skinned" Dravidians to the south, settling down in the rich Ganges Valley.

Their scriptures, the Vedas, were probably completed by 500 B.C. They were written in Sanskrit, which is still the sacred language of the Hindus. Indeed, many of the religious beliefs and philosophic ideas of Hinduism can be traced back to the Vedas.

Two other religions also arose in ancient India. These were Jainism and Buddhism and both were protests against the philosophic mysticism of the Vedic religion. Both new faiths maintained that every man had to work out his own salvation from bondage to the laws of karma and rebirth by strenuous self-discipline. Today there are very few Buddhists left in India, but in contrast, Jainism, which never extended beyond the land of its origin, still claims the allegiance of some million and a half believers. It is perhaps most noteworthy for its doctrine of *ahimsa*, the principle of non-injury to life in any form.

Until the eleventh century the vast subcontinent of India was ruled by many rajas, or kings, whose territories were more or less independent. Periodically one among them exercised lordship over wide regions, but never for long. Within each kingdom there was comparative peace and order. The village was the unit of government, and agriculture and cottage industries were the mainstay of an economy in which each village tended to be self-sufficient. There was, however, considerable trade. Cotton, spices, and precious stones were exported to other parts of the then-known world. This foreign commerce was moved by sail from the west coast of India, or by caravan across the northwest mountain passes.

Largely attracted by these exports, hordes of invaders descended on India near the beginning of the eleventh century. Soon much of the country was overrun. The most powerful of the conquering Muslim groups were the Moguls, who established their dynasty in Delhi in 1526 and dominated the history of the subcontinent for almost three hundred years. The Muslim rulers were often intolerant. Opposed to idolatry, they destroyed and plundered many Hindu temples and in the early periods put many people to the sword.

Muhammad, the founder of Islam, had taught that Allah, the one true God, was the sovereign God of all mankind. Everyone was to submit to him and him alone. This stern monotheism did not tolerate Hindu polytheism. Muslims also believed that the faithful formed one brotherhood in which all were regarded as equal. The Hindu idea of many castes was abhorrent to them. The elaborate temple worship of Hinduism, its priestly offerings, its many religious observances, and its many sacred sayings were repugnant. Muslims believed in a simple form of prayer said five times a day. Once a week they assembled in the mosque, said their prayer as a congregation, and listened to a sermon based on the words of their scripture, the Koran. The Muslim scripture, a simple volume of revealed truth, stood in vivid contrast to the philosophical subtleties of the voluminous sacred literature of the Hindus.

Although the Muslim rulers denounced the Hinduism of their subjects, there was considerable mutual cultural influence during the nearly seven centuries of their connection with India. In part this was due to the fact that many Muslims married Hindu women; in part also to the scholarly interest that the educated classes took in each other's sacred literature. Saint worship was commonly accepted by ordinary Muslims, among whom a sort of caste system also became prevalent. Hindus in turn came to see the evils of caste and the significance of personal devotion as against temple ritual. The Hindu aristocracy adopted the ways and manners of their Muslim counterparts.

The most notable outcome of the interaction between Hinduism and Islam, however, was the rise of a new religion, Sikhism. Founded by the Hindu teacher, Nanak (1469–1538), it combined Muslim monotheism and Hindu mystical devotion. Nanak opposed idolatry and caste and accepted neither the Vedas nor the Koran. Sikhism did not become popular either among Hindus or Muslims. In fact the Muslims took a virulent dislike to the Sikhs, persecuting them severely in the Punjab, which was their stronghold. The result was that the Sikhs became organized as a military community and eventually set up a strong Sikh kingdom that waged war against the Muslim rulers and the rising new power of the British.

The British, like the other European powers, came as traders in the wake of Vasco da Gama, who had rounded the Cape of Good Hope and found his way to Calicut on the west coast of India in 1498. The trade settlements established by the British East India Company became garrisoned forts; and before the British Government fully realized what was happening, it found itself taking sides in the wars and quarrels of the local rajas. By the beginning of the nineteenth century, Great Britain had become the paramount power throughout the subcontinent, and in 1877 Queen Victoria was crowned Empress of India.

Under British rule, India made tremendous progress. Law and order were established throughout the land by an efficient corps of civil servants. Railroads were built; postal and telegraph services were introduced; agriculture was improved; highways were constructed; and education, through the medium of the English language, became widespread. All this was not intended by the government to benefit its subjects. The imperial power reaped enormous profits through trade—buying cheap raw material from the Indians and selling them British manufactured goods. India also paid heavily for the British civil service and the army, in both of which Indians could be employed only in subordinate offices. Although there were periods of liberalism and reform, it became increasingly apparent that Britain ruled India for the benefit of the rulers, not the ruled. From the beginning of the twentieth century, Indian leaders began agitating, first for a representative government and for appointment to state offices, then for Dominion status, and finally for freedom and self-government.

The freedom struggle, which the Indian National Congress under the leadership of Mahatma Gāndhi had started in 1920, grew steadily apace. Gāndhi's non-violent non-co-operation, the boycott of British goods, and the spreading discontent that reached out to the village folk seriously embarrassed the government. Gāndhi was supported by able leaders like Sardar Vallabhbhia Patel, Chakravarti Rajagopalacharia, Rajendra Prasad, and Jawaharlal Nehru among a host of others. At first Muslim leaders also joined in the agitation, but if the growing spirit of nationalism united opposition against British rule, it also intensified the basic differences between Hindus and Muslims. Mounting communal tension led the Muslim League to espouse self-determination for the Muslim communities in the late thirties. By the close of the second world war, Mohammed Ali Jinnah, the spokesman for the Muslim League, was urging a separate Islamic state. India teetered on the brink of civil war. Unable to secure agreement from the two contending groups, Great Britain announced her intention to transfer her power to two governments instead of one. The two separate states of India and Pakistan came into being on August 15, 1947.

Partition only momentarily halted the communal strife. Soon millions of Hindus were fleeing in terror from Pakistan and millions of Muslims from India. Riots broke out in the Punjab and Bengal. For a time violence and bloodshed cast their fearful shadows over both countries. It is calculated that during the terrible six weeks of madness nearly a million and a half people met with untimely death, much property was damaged, and millions of people were uprooted and left homeless and penniless. There was a momentary lull, but strife probably would have begun again if a strange thing had not happened to shake the whole subcontinent. During the weeks of terrible violence, Mahatma Gāndhi had resorted to fasting to bring about Hindu-Muslim concord. His action had enraged Hindu extremists who believed that he was a party to the vivisection of Mother India. For his effort he paid with his life. He was assassinated by a Hindu fanatic as he was walking in the Birla House grounds in Delhi on the way to lead his usual evening prayer meeting. That was on January 30, 1948, and Gāndhi was seventy-eight years of age. People on both sides of the border came to their senses. The worst was over, although more subdued crowds of refugees still trekked across the border for some time to come. It is heartening to recall that many Christian social service agencies, led by the National Christian Council, gave unstinting service to Hindu and Muslim alike in the hastily established refugee camps.

The nightmare did not last for long. Both India and Pakistan plunged into the task of nation building, and the process is still going on. After all, sixteen years does not count for much in a nation's annals. However, the progress made within this brief span of time is nothing less than revolutionary.

India declared herself a secular democratic republic and has successfully held three general elections. Jawaharlal Nehru as Prime Minister and leader of the Congress party has guided the affairs of the country with singular success these sixteen years. A series of five-year-plans for national development have encompassed land reform, promotion of industry, improvement of road transport, spread of literacy and education, rural reconstruction, and social progress. All this has been uphill work. Foreign aid in the form of technical assistance and substantial loans, especially from the United States, has been of enormous help in implementing the development plans.

Pakistan chose to become an Islamic state within the

British Commonwealth. In 1958 the constitution was annulled and the nation was put under martial law. Gen. Mohammed Ayub Khan assumed control when the president resigned. General elections confirmed Khan in power and he was sworn in as president in 1960. A new constitution allowing for more village participation is now being drafted.

A sweeping land reform program and sound economic measures are helping Pakistan recover from an initially slow start. Here also generous foreign aid from the United States has helped national reorganization and economic development.

The vexing question of the future of the northern state of Kashmir—claimed by both India and Pakistan—has been hanging fire, and until that issue is amicably settled, the relation between these two countries will continue to be strained. But the fact that in India there are nearly 4 million Muslims alongside of about 372 million Hindus and that in Pakistan there are 12 million Hindus and 80 million Muslims makes it inevitable that the two neighbor states should establish closer ties, especially in view of the background of their common cultural and social heritage.

CHAPTER 2

The Church Comes to India

THE St. Thomas Church in South India is one of the most ancient churches in the world. Tradition traces its founding back to St. Thomas, the Apostle, whose martyred remains are supposed to be buried in a church in Mylepore, near Madras. Whatever the truth about St. Thomas, there is little doubt that from as early as the fourth century, there were scattered groups of Christians in India and a colony in Kerala, whose founders probably had come originally from Syria.

These early Christians lived in comparative isolation from other Christians until the arrival of the Portuguese in the fifteenth century. They had little understanding of their faith and did not acknowledge the authority of the Pope, being historically related to the Nestorians of Mesopotamia. In 1599 a synod at Udiamperur, called by the Roman Catholic Archbishop of Goa, persuaded the entire community of St. Thomas Christians (or Syrian Christians as they are sometimes known) to accept the Pope as the head of their church. Soon after the synod, the Archbishop took stern measures to force the Roman confession and church discipline on both clergy and laity alike.

The new ways of worship and church order were strange and unacceptable to the St. Thomas Christians. Sixty years after Udiamperur dissenting clergy organized a mass protest, renouncing Roman jurisdiction. They took a vast majority of their people back to the Syriac rites and church order, consecrating one of their own number as Bishop. Some time in the seventeenth century a number of these Christians abandoned their own rites, established relations with the Jacobite Patriarch of Antioch, and thenceforth came to be known as Jacobites. Today, besides those Christians who adhered to Rome, there are two groups, one owing allegiance to the Patriarch and the other acknowledging only their local Metropolitan as head of the church. These latter are really a reform group known as the Mar Thoma Syrian Church. They have pronounced evangelical views and place considerable emphasis on mission work.

The Syrian Christians of Kerala are highly educated and economically advanced. They have provided a great deal of leadership for the church in other parts of India as well. So far, however, they have lived as something of a caste group, very rarely marrying outside their own community and more or less confined to their ancestral state.

ROMAN CATHOLICISM

The Roman church is now widespread in India, and of the over eight and one-half million Christians in the country more than half are Roman Catholic. Nearly three-quarters of the Catholics are found in Kerala, Madras, and Goa. An archbishop has resided in Goa, except for a very short period, ever since 1534.

The names of Francis Xavier (1506–1552) and Robert de Nobili (1577–1656) are held in great reverence by Indian Catholics. Xavier labored among the low-caste fisher folk in Tuticorin. De Nobili worked in Madura among the high-caste Brahmans. Just as the objects of their evangelism were different, so also were the methods of the two men. One emphasized the need for bringing caste communities into the church by group conversion, however ill-prepared they were for baptism. Their

Christian nurture, he held, began only after they had been brought into the church. The other pressed the point that Christianity should be adapted to Hindu religious institutions and philosophic expressions if the higher castes were to be won for Christ. So de Nobili put on the saffron robes of an ascetic, gave up eating meat, and put his cross on a sacred thread such as the Brahmans wore. He mastered the Sanskrit language and ventured on public disputations with Hindu scholars of the day, using the texts of the Hindu scriptures to preach the gospel.

There are values and dangers in both these methods of evangelism, and Indian Christianity, both Roman Catholic and Protestant, has been grappling with the issues involved ever since the days of these missionary pioneers.

The Portuguese undoubtedly believed that by making the people Christian, by whatever means, they could strengthen their colonial power. Little attention was paid to the spiritual growth of the early converts. Many of them merely accepted the outward ways and manners of their missionary fathers, showing little indication in their lives of any real change as a result of their new faith.

This political motivation was one of the main reasons why all the early efforts of Portuguese missionary pioneers to make converts among the high-caste Hindus proved futile. When they did make converts among the Brahmans, the new Christians maintained their caste behavior. The common practice until a few years ago of having different places of worship for high-caste and low-caste Catholics, or admitting only people of high-caste origin to the priesthood, is evidence of the danger in "adaptation." Moreover, by giving in on this question of caste, the Roman Church also permitted a number of other Hindu religious customs that could not be reconciled with Christian beliefs.

After Portuguese power waned in Southern Asia, Roman Catholic missions were increasingly manned by French and Italian priests. But the change made little difference until the beginning of the nineteenth century when the church began to grow, especially in South India. Since then, and particularly at the beginning of this century, the Roman Catholic Church has registered remarkable progress. After the second world war and possibly as a result of withdrawal from China, the work in India has been greatly strengthened by additional funds and personnel. This has been reflected in the many new educational institutions built within the last fifteen years in both India and Pakistan.

First-rate educational institutions for boys and girls and well-equipped colleges have been the primary aim of Roman missions. These schools have been responsible for the growth of an able Catholic laity, some members of which are holding important positions in government and the professions. From these institutions also have come most of the clergy, who are in some ways better equipped than are the Protestant ministers. A 1961 report shows that three-fourths of the nearly six thousand priests are Indian and nearly two thousand more are being prepared for the priesthood in major Indian seminaries. The report also discloses that there are 16,000 Indian nuns.

Another development is the rapid nationalization of the hierarchy. Thirteen of the fifteen archbishops, including a cardinal, are Indians. Of the forty-nine dioceses, twenty-eight are directed by Indian bishops. This preponderance of nationals is also true of Ceylon and Pakistan. In this respect Roman Catholics are ahead of the Protestants, largely because they have given importance to the training of leaders, but also because no budgetary measures are involved in the transfer of leadership. In the Protestant churches every time a national is "promoted" to a place occupied by a foreign missionary it involves also a "raise" in salary and allowance. Again, the provision for pastoral care of Catholic congregations is more adequate and better organized than that of Protestant groups.

In the expansion of the Roman Church during the early nineteenth century, there was some unwholesome rivalry with Protestant groups and a certain amount of "sheep stealing." Protestant missions were also culpable in this matter. But as the century wore out there was less and less of this tendency. Today there is no trace of it on the part of the Catholics, although Protestant sectarian groups still persist in such proselytism. In India and Ceylon it is not unusual for Catholic bishops to be present and sometimes to participate in gatherings with other Christians. Catholic clergy frequently join in study conferences on social issues with non-Christian faiths.

There is undoubtedly developing in the larger city areas in all these countries of Southern Asia something more than mere tolerance. There is a determined effort to understand the differences in the theological positions of Roman Catholics and Protestants, an organized move to stand together on national issues specifically confronting the Christian minority, and an increasing willingness to work together in new patterns of service, wherever it is possible. For example, when Ceylon announced its plans for the reorganization of education, and the future of private schools was at stake, Roman Catholic and Protestant educators got together and discussed their common problems. And when the Indian state of Kerala was passing through a crisis under a Communist government, Catholic, Protestant, and Orthodox Christians worked together.

One other thing must be said for the Roman Church. Since World War II it has taken the call to social action very seriously, especially in India and in Ceylon. Catholic centers have been established for thorough study by experts of the social problems confronting the new nations. Through church groups and youth organizations, active steps are being taken to interest the laity in civic and social reform so that Christians can make a vital impact on the nation's life. So far, however, this latter aspect of the Christian mission has not progressed very much beyond the study stage, being still more the concern of the clergy than of the laity.

PROTESTANT BEGINNINGS

The first Protestant missionaries, Bartholomaus Ziegenbalg and Heinrich Plutschau, landed in a small Danish settlement called Tranquebar in South India on July 9, 1706. Two hundred and fifty years later this historic event was celebrated throughout Christian India with great enthusiasm.

Learning the local language is a first requirement for every missionary wherever he goes. In those days, when there were no dictionaries, no textbooks for beginners, and no simplified manuals of grammar, learning a foreign language was a stupendous task. It is a marvel how these missionary pioneers did it, especially when one learns of the dictionaries they compiled and the classics they translated. Another requirement was to get the translations into print as fast as possible. But printing was a cumbersome business. For one thing, the type in these various alphabets had to be cut; for another thing the machinery had to be imported and reassembled. When we are told that the first printed copies of the New Testament came out of the little mission press in Tranquebar in the year 1714, just eight years after the first two missionaries landed, it sounds unbelievable.

Of the missionaries who came after Plutschau and Ziegenbalg, perhaps the most famous was Christian Friedrich Schwartz. He arrived in India in 1750 and traveled extensively, preaching the gospel to the Hindus and nurturing the faith of the little congregations that had by now come into being in many towns such as Trichinopoly and Tanjore (Thanjavur). It was Schwartz, and his Indian fellow-worker, Sathyanadhan, who ventured out to the southernmost part of India, Tinnevelly (Tirunelveli), and began work there. That field was to yield great harvest in the years to come. In the first half of the nineteenth century whole villages became Christian, and today there are three hundred thousand Christians in Tirunelveli.

By caste origin the social standing of these first converts was low; their profession was the manufacture of a kind of strong liquor from the juice of the palmyra palm. But they took eagerly to education, and the books they learned best were the Bible and the Prayer Book. Today their descendants are found literally by the thousands in high government offices, business concerns, industrial firms, and the learned professions. That is not all. For well over a century these Christian families have provided devoted ministers and lay evangelists for the entire church in South India. And their leadership has extended beyond India. The first Indian bishop of the Anglican church, the earliest of ecumenical leaders from India, V. S. Azariah, was from Tirunelveli, only two generations removed from the first wave of mass movement converts in this field.

One interesting fact about these missionary pioneers of the line of Ziegenbalg and Schwartz should be mentioned. They were of German origin, Lutheran by confession, sponsored by a pious Danish king, and supported by the Society for Promoting Christian Knowledge (S.P.C.K.), which was an English organization! What is now called the ecumenical movement owes its origin to the missionary movement. The mission of the church is best carried out together.

The next great missionary pioneer, the English Baptist William Carey, also started work in a Danish settlement. The British East India Company, which governed for the Crown, opposed any missionary work being done in British territory. As a consequence, Carey was forced to leave Calcutta, where he had landed in 1793, and to seek sanctuary of the Danish governor of Serampore. This center became famous in mission annals for its wide-ranging activities under Carey's direction. He was, in a real sense, the father of modern missions.

Meanwhile, the British East India Company was compelled to alter its policies. The company had opposed Christian work among its Hindu and Muslim subjects because it feared that any interference with religious beliefs and practices might lead to trouble. However, Christian opinion in England was becoming convinced that the gospel should be preached wherever there was an opportunity to do so. Thus in 1813 an act of Parliament required the East India Company to let down its barriers to Christian missions. Given this right of entry, many courageous men and women set out from Britain, Europe, and the United States to preach the gospel to the Hindus, Buddhists, and Muslims of Southern Asia.

In every case, the pioneering task was the same: laborious study of the language, painstaking translation of the Christian Scriptures, careful research of the sacred literature of the people to whom the gospel was preached, and the beginning of little congregations of the newly-baptized.

The second stage, after the pioneering first steps had been taken, involved ventures into the field of education, particularly higher education. Carey himself was the first to see the need for this, and other men who followed—Alexander Duff in Calcutta, John Wilson in Bombay, William Miller in Madras—were all convinced that if the higher castes were to be won over to the faith it would be through education. The local governments encouraged such study, and many high-caste youth joined these Christian colleges because a sound English education was a passport to employment and the new world of Western knowledge.

The Christian schools and colleges provided a unique opportunity for the missionary teacher to impart instruction in the faith to Hindu and Muslim youth through Bible study and daily worship. The amazing success of this evangelistic method in the early days of the Christian missionary enterprise was most encouraging. Many Brahman and high-caste youth joined the church—all the way from Lahore (now in Pakistan) down to Tirunelveli in southern India, and on to Jaffna, Ceylon.

This early wave of conversions did not last long, however. The new scientific education of the time, which was expected to expose the weakness of non-Christian faiths, also placed emphasis on rationalism, humanism, and materialism. Everything had to be put to the final test of reason. The highest good for which people could work was the welfare of man. Progress and prosperity were dependent on material things. If the lands of Southern Asia were less advanced and more poverty-stricken, the people in these countries should do something about these conditions. Educated people began thinking in terms of freedom and social and economic reform. With the beginning of the twentieth century, the rising tide of nationalism captured the imagination of youth.

CHRISTIAN CONTRIBUTIONS

It is true that Christian education in mission schools and colleges did not result in many conversions. But it produced generations of graduates, both men and women, who were fired with zeal for service to their fellowmen; people who were sensitive to injustice, suffering, and want. Many missionary educators themselves felt that Christian education should be directed to such ends. Not that they minimized the role of Christian colleges in Christian evangelism but that they accepted an interpretation of evangelism in the wider sense of bringing people under the influence of Christian social values and Christian attitudes toward life.

It was believed that Christian schools and colleges in Southern Asia should help develop trained leadership for the Christian communities. Although this purpose was realized in great measure, more and more emphasis is now being given to leadership training that is not solely limited to the Christian minorities. In Pakistan, for instance, mission schools are helping the state in its widespread education and literacy program. It may be that in Nepal, too, the door will be opened for some such service by Christian educators, although with certain restrictions on religious education. In India, however, the needs of the Christian community are still paramount. This does not necessarily mean more educational institutions but rather well-equipped student centers and hostels, maintained in close association with secular colleges. The situation in Ceylon is in a state of flux at the moment, since education has become a governmental responsibility. Although private schools are tolerated, they are not permitted to charge any fees and must submit to a periodic check by the state. There are also restrictions on religious education, the pupils can only be taught in the religion of their upbringing. Many Christian schools, buildings and equipment, have been taken over by the state, without any compensation, because the church could not afford to run them as private schools. Only a handful are now being maintained, and how long they can be kept is open to question. The Ceylon education program has also created widespread opposition with some rioting among the Hindu Tamils.

Although additions to the church in India were very slow and discouraging in the early decades of the nineteenth century, there was a phenomenal rise in membership during the last decades of that century. This was true almost everywhere in the countries of Southern Asia. The rapid growth was due to the fact that many low-caste folk became Christians in large groups, the decision being made by the caste leaders.

Several reasons led the leaders to take such a step. Caste oppression made life miserable. There was no way, except by getting out of Hinduism, for scavengers or cobblers or landless serfs to escape the tyranny of the Hindu customs that held them down in their helpless state. As Christians, they had an opportunity for education, better living, and self-respect. Christianity was a religion that did not countenance gruesome animal sacrifices to dreaded spirits. It talked of love, forgiveness, and purity. It insisted on honest dealing, prayerful devotion, and absolute trust in a God who cared for the simple and the lowly. The people did not understand all the teachings of the Bible that they heard, but the story of the Lord Jesus gripped their hearts and minds.

Perhaps the first generation of these mass movement converts did not fully grasp the far-flung consequences of their actions. But the results can be measured in the third and fourth generations. What these results were to be, depended on the care and diligence of the missionary and his colleagues. Boarding schools, where the children of these mass movement converts were given a Christian education in an atmosphere totally different from the caste-ridden village, made for revolutionary change. Worship became meaningful, the Word of God spoke to their condition, personal habits were transformed. But it did not happen in every case. Not often the third generation became indifferent; they were satisfied with being nominal Christians. However, it justly may be claimed that the gains far outweighed the losses.

There are still periodic accessions to the church in Southern Asia through group conversions, although they are not so frequent nor as spectacularly numerous as in the earlier period. The reasons for the decline are many. Governments have taken active measures to remove caste disabilities. In India discrimination on the basis of caste origin is a penal offense. Education, modern industry, land reform, and community development plans have radically changed conditions for many. The state has more resources for material aid to the socially underprivileged than missions and churches can command. Moreover, Hindu and Buddhist religious leaders are now making serious effort to reclaim these once neglected people by throwing open temples, reviving village shrines, and severely discountenancing all gruesome animal sacrifices.

Since 1900 Christian missions in Southern Asia have been interested in public health and rural welfare. From the beginning of Christian missions there had been some medical work, of course. But trained medical missionaries were recruited only when it was found that a great deal of evangelism could be done through regular hospitals and dispensaries. People who came for medical aid were not only treated for their bodily illness, they were told about the Great Physician. They joined in Christian worship. They talked to the Christian physician and the nurses about God, suffering, sin, and death. But these hospitals had to be equipped and maintained with up-to-date appliances and expert staff. All this was expensive business, and it was not always possible to secure nationals who were both qualified and willing to serve in mission hospitals. Besides, governments were rapidly extending their health services.

After the second world war, and the growth of international organizations generously supported by secular foundations, it became increasingly clear that the church should not attempt to do more than it could in this field. The decision of the churches to concentrate on two aspects of Christian medical work was a wise and necessary one. The first emphasis was on the training of a corps of efficient nurses. And today many young women in Southern Asia are turning to this profession. The second emphasis was on united sponsorship of thoroughly good medical schools. In Vellore, India, such an institution has been developed. Carefully selected students, both men and women, are given excellent training for academic degrees awarded by the University of Madras. Ludhiana, in the Punjab, also offers such solid training.

Other fields include rural medicine and public health education in co-operation with government agencies. The church also has done a great deal for the treatment and control of leprosy and tuberculosis.

Rural reconstruction came to be accepted as another field of service for the church after the close of the first world war. Much of the impetus for this work was given by the Indian Christian YMCA leader, K. T. Paul. About the same time Sam Higginbottom, in Allahabad, and Jack De Valois, in Katpadi, started agricultural institutes to help promote training in modern methods of farming. These Christian pioneers in agriculture could not do very much with their limited means, but they did help to awaken others who took up their cause. Eventually the governments themselves became concerned. Especially since their independence, India and Pakistan have made vast strides in the planning and construction of huge hydroelectric systems for irrigation and power. Plans for co-operative farming, the development of cottage industries so that the farmer can add to his meager income, and increased mechanization are all part of these programs. Caught up in what has been called the "revolution of rising expectations," the Southern Asian farmer is no longer content to till his soil and tend his crops in the primitive fashion of his ancestors.

CHAPTER 3

The Mission Becomes the Church

THE immediate outcome of missionary work is the gathering together of a group of converts to the faith. Small congregations of Christians come into being. They are organized for worship and fellowship under the pastoral care of the missionary. They gather together periodically in a place of worship, where they are instructed in the faith and prepared to receive the sacrament. They are taught to bring their offerings and learn to support the congregation. In time they also participate in the ordering of the life of the

Christian community and in witness to their non-Christian neighbors.

These characteristic stages in the evolution of the local church may be summarized as follows: a worshiping community; a teacher-catechist to be succeeded in time by an ordained pastor; regular instruction leading to membership through receiving the Holy Communion; training in stewardship toward self-support and self-government; Christian witness with a view to self-propagation and the extension of the kingdom. In this way the mission grows to maturity and becomes the church in that place.

In the countries of Southern Asia, there are congregations in *all* these stages of development. Most are still in the earlier stages. Only a few have come to be self-supporting, self-governing, and self-propagating congregations. Of course, it is true that the local congregation is also the local manifestation of the church in that land. And it is proper to talk about the church in India, in Pakistan, in Ceylon, and so forth. But easy generalizations may distort the true picture. The situation is complex because conditions in particular congregations differ. The situation is also dynamic because every congregation is moving, often unevenly, from stage to stage. Nevertheless, missions are giving place to the church in each land. A partial achievement is an achievement just the same.

As congregations, progressing through the various stages of development, succeed the missions and become the churches, new relationships between the mission home lands and the overseas or "younger" churches are evolving. Christians are learning to think of the church as a reality wherever it is—not in terms of where it came from. What is really happening is that the entire Christian world is becoming increasingly conscious of Christ as the center of its total life. The immediate problem for Christians everywhere is to realize themselves as part of God's people in a world of his making.

FACTORS AFFECTING CHURCH GROWTH

This growth of the church can really be looked at from two viewpoints. On the one hand, the change from missions to churches in the local perspective is a view of congregational growth from infant Christian communities to self-supporting, self-governing, and self-propagating local churches. On the other hand, from the world perspective, the change from missions to churches is a change of relationship between the "older" and "younger" churches—a progress from dependence to interdependence.

Another factor affecting the growth of the church is the great awakening that has swept over Asian lands during the last one hundred years. It has found expression in many ways. Perhaps the most noticeable has been on a political level. With the rise of nationalism, Asian peoples asserted their right to be free to manage their own affairs, vigorously protesting against domination by European powers. Nationalism, however, is but one aspect of the Asian revival. Also to be taken into account are the social reform, the cultural renaissance, and the religious resurgence that are likewise part of the national awakening.

Traditional social institutions prevailing in South Asia have been found increasingly unsuitable for modern life. The caste structure has been rudely shaken throughout the area. The position of women in society has changed. A sense of pride is growing for the cultural heritage of centuries. The new interest in the study of local languages and the rich literature of some has given rise to demands for a replacement of English, which was long the common medium of communication and the language of public administration. And not to be overlooked, of course, is the resurgence of Hinduism in India, of Islam in Pakistan, and of Buddhism in Ceylon.

Throughout the period of the growth of the church in this part of the world, these three forces of change—the emergence of the church from the mission, the changing relationship between the younger and the older churches, and the widespread national awakening—have been increasingly at work. The consequences have been tremendous. Nothing like planned development has been possible, but the general lines of progress may be traced in terms of certain specific objectives.

Foremost of these, from the very beginning, has been the goal of building up local congregations that could meet regularly for worship and fellowship. In almost every village of any importance, in practically all the small towns, and certainly in the larger cities of India, Pakistan, and Ceylon there are now worshiping congregations.

Not all congregations have churches and pastors of their own. Especially in the villages, they meet in a schoolhouse or a thatched shed set apart for the purpose. A local teacher conducts the worship. Periodically, and that may be once a month or once in three months, an ordained minister comes to administer the Holy Communion. The congregations in these small villages can scarcely afford to give anything to the church, much less toward the support of the lay worker. By and large, the people are illiterate, and the oral instruction given them at the hours of worship has to be elementary. Still, the numbers grow, in some places rapidly, in other places very slowly.

In vivid contrast are the town congregations. These Christians are mostly of middle-class background—doctors, lawyers, government employees, teachers, and other professional men and women. They are anglicized in their ways and manners, and their church life is patterned on models that prevail in Europe or America. During worship, the hymns and prayers, the sermon, and the announcements may all be in the local language but still adhere rigidly to the original English or German forms. Strangely enough the church records and the affairs of the parish committees are kept in English. The church buildings, too, are markedly different from village places of worship. They are built like those of the Western world with pews and pulpit, altar and chancel, choir stall and organ loft. The ministers are usually university men, trained in theological schools of good standing.

These urbanized middle-class folk are in fact the grandchildren and the great-grandchildren of village Christians. But for some two generations they have grown up in a totally different environment. They no longer have any contact with their village relatives. Their forebears left their village homes for good when they came out in search of an education, employment, and better living conditions. Mission high schools, colleges, and hospitals were built in towns and cities, and this widened still further the gulf between village and urban Christians. Perhaps, too, the church in Southern Asia has been tending to become middle class and urban in order to forget its outcaste rural origin.

With the comparative neglect of the village folk, expansion of the church has suffered. Instead of venturing out in courage and faith to discover new ways and means of spreading the Good News in areas of need, Asian Christians have been devoting too much attention to consolidating their gains by building up the organizational life of urban Christian congregations.

National leaders in Asian lands are beginning to realize that rural needs demand high priority in state action. Independence had set such immediate tasks as constitution making, internal reorganization, development of foreign political and business ties, economic planning, and the like. These urgent concerns absorbed attention until now when it is being recognized that governmental reorganization is not enough. The needs of the people still grow apace. The common man in Southern Asia still lives in the village, where he is beset by caste restrictions, illiteracy, poverty, land tenure problems, inefficient methods of agriculture, and a fatalistic view of life. Government spokesmen of the various countries insist that redoubled efforts must be made to carry the rural folk along with their nations in the rapid march toward progress.

Christian Asians, however, seem to be in danger of ignoring the call of the rural folk that comes with a new urgency. The need of the hour is for Christian concern to concentrate creative effort in the village once again, as it did in an earlier generation. Only as the message of the gospel is preached afresh to the village and bears fruit can we Asians be faithful in our Christian mission. There is a pressing need for widespread literacy and rural education that will help our people not only to read and write but to acquire the modern skills necessary for making a living in their rural setting. The witness of Christian faith—creating among the villagers a new sense of human worth as the children of God for whom Christ died—can only be demonstrated if Christian teachers, welfare workers, doctors, and nurses choose to live as Christians, not as mission employees, among and with the village people. Then the local congregation would become spotlighted as a center of Christian inspiration and community witness. The leaven of Christian influence in any community works not through isolated testimony of individual faith but through the corporate witness of the transformed group in fellowship with their Living Lord. Under such circumstances, evangelism assumes a new form; the gospel becomes relevant, faith is communicated in the living encounter with unbelief, and the church takes firm root in the soil to work its creative change in the lives of the people.

Another factor affecting the growth of the church in Southern Asia has been interpreted in terms of autonomy and freedom. Not only Asian Christians but also those abroad ask such questions as this: Would the church in India become truly Indian if it became completely independent of foreign assistance in men and money? The question has practical bearings, especially now that India is an independent country. Indians are no longer under the control of foreigners. The day-to-day administration of government, at all levels, is in our own hands. Foreign personnel is secured only for technical assistance, to do for us what we like done but find we are not now sufficiently skilled to do ourselves. Money is also accepted from other people as "foreign aid" to carry out some of these plans, but on the understanding that no strings are to be attached to such grants.

It is natural for Christians in Southern Asia to think that this same policy, in the main, should apply to their churches, if they are to be free and independent. But what is not sufficiently realized is that the underlying factor involved in a nation and its freedom is the government itself, the way it carries on its administration and provides for the welfare of the people. It is true that the church also is something of an organized institution. It has its legislative bodies, its machinery of administration, and its plans for maintaining service organizations both for the Christian community and the country at large. Unfortunately, it is also true that this governmental aspect of the church—which we have an easy way of wrongly describing as missions—was for many years in the hands of foreign missionaries, maintained by foreign money. In some areas of the world this is still so.

MISSIONS AND THE CHURCH

With the best of intentions, efforts have been made to free the local church from the control of the mission. This process has been called "devolution," that is, step by step, the affairs of the local churches have been handed over to local councils controlled by nationals. But the work of the mission board, which consisted of projects for which men and money were needed, was retained in the hands of missionary committees. These committees were usually directed by foreign missionaries or their representatives. The plan seemed to work well for some time. Local churches developed initiative and leadership, became more self-supporting and self-governing. They raised their own money to pay for their clergy and to maintain their church buildings. Sometimes they even took care of secondary schools with the help they got from grants-in-aid given by the government. But in this fatal division of responsibilities, the mission board continued to be responsible for evangelism, the preaching of the gospel to the non-Christian. The task of Christian witness, whether through institutions or through an organized campaign to communicate the Good News by word and deed, was not given to the local church. Because of this division, local congregations and many church councils have come to accept the idea that evangelism is not their concern. They need only to take care of their church life, to pay their clergy, and to keep their buildings in good repair.

To check this evil, there is now a belated movement to integrate mission and church. But such integration is in terms of unification of administration and the substitution of national for foreign leaders on mission committees. The unhappy division still remains between church and mission, aggravated by the fact that the division now is within the younger church itself.

All this experience has been illuminating, for in the process Christians have come to realize what is the church and what the mission. What is more, they are realizing that the church is mission. There is also a growing understanding of the real significance of such words as freedom, nationalism, indigenous, and foreign when they are applied to the church and its mission. Surely these terms cannot have the same meaning to Christians as to the secular world. A great deal of misunderstanding and heartache could have been avoided if we Christians, Asian and Western, had first set about defining some of these confusing words that mean different things in different contexts.

For instance, is the church free just because the church government is in the hands of nationals? To what extent does the church in any land become national and indigenous? Can the church as the church ever cease to be foreign, especially in Asian lands where Christians will continue to be a minority? More than all, if the church exists because of the mission to proclaim the gospel, if that mission is "the whole mission of the whole church to the whole world," and if all are involved in mission together, it seems wrong to think of national and non-national in terms of men and money. And yet the church in every land is indigenous and national!

The point is this: the whole question of the place of the foreign missionary as well as the question of dependence on foreign money should be answered without mixing up these issues with the prevailing contemporary sentiment about nationalism, freedom, and colonialism. Otherwise we Christians would be admitting the charge that the church and its mission is determined by the politics of the more powerful Christian nations. Whatever the evidence of history, and however much the purely human factor is determinative in Christian decisions, there should be an unceasing effort to seek and find answers to these issues in terms of the church and its mission. This does not mean that we should not think in the context of our times, we can scarcely do otherwise. But the situation in which we find ourselves should not totally condition our thinking.

Looked at from this point of view, the question resolves itself into another: Are we Asian Christians getting the most out of the foreign personnel that works with us, and are we putting to wise and effective use the money that we get from foreign sources? The people who come to help and the monies they bring are meant to strengthen the churches so that they become increasingly self-reliant, truly rooted in the soil, and vitally conscious of their mission to witness to the non-Christian world around them. Are foreign personnel and foreign support utilized to contribute to these ends? Or is it possible that we are using these God-given resources— made so plentiful at a time when the church's opportunity seems at its peak in the history of our people— toward ends that further our communal isolation, our cultural apartness, and our "mission compound" interest? The responsibility falls this time upon us of the Asian churches, and it calls for some frank self-examination.

"We are concerned with the shaping of the future of India. It is therefore with a sense of the burden of history upon me, upon us, upon this house, that I face this problem," observed Prime Minister Nehru of India recently. He was opening the debate in the Indian Parliament on the Second Five Year Plan. The sense of the burden of history is the new awareness of cultural heritage. Under foreign rule and influence, our future was being planned for us by others without reference to our past. Today as a free people we are busy building anew, but on foundations already laid.

This new self-awareness is not only true of India but

of all countries in freshly awakened Asia and Africa. Political freedom has brought to the new nations a sense of pride in their own cultural heritages. At the same time, there is a widespread acceptance of modern social and economic values, due to the increasing impact of industrialization. Out of the interplay of these two contradictory forces, traditional culture is itself being restated by a process of creative selection. Thus the burden of history resolves itself into a dynamic urge for cultural change and social re-patterning. The problem is to conserve the traditional values that are worth preserving while reinterpreting them to meet the new demands of present history.

ISSUES FOR ASIAN CHRISTIANS

In these countries Christian congregations that are of recent origin are also facing the same problem of cultural revolution, but in a different way. For various reasons, after we became Christians, we lived in comparative isolation, a group apart from the rest of the people. But today the burden of history lies heavily on us, too. We are faced with the question of how best we can recover our cultural identity and sense of national belonging without losing what we have gained in our Christian faith and fellowship.

What gives concern is not so much the foreignness of our faith but the fact that Christian people, by and large, do not seem to be involved in the surging current of new life. Differences in religious beliefs and practices are accepted. What estranges us from our people is our way of life, our introverted social relationships, our lack of civic concern. We Asian Christians thus find ourselves outside the larger whole of the national community.

How can we as Christian people become rooted in the nation? That is the question, not how to make Christianity indigenous. It is clear that the faith of the Christian, which is centered in the gospel of Jesus Christ, cannot be made indigenous to any one national culture. What should become part of the environment is not the gospel but the people who are committed to the claims of that gospel and who want to witness to the truth of it in the very environment of which they are a part.

Christians in the lands of the younger churches are faced with three distinguishable issues. The first is that of recovering their sense of identity with their fellow-countrymen. This consists not only in wholehearted participation in nation building but also in re-establishing cultural kinship with their people. It implies two things at the same time. One is to discard foreign customs and manners, and the other is to return to attitudes and standards characteristic of their neighbors. In India, for instance, most Christians are westernized in their clothes, in the food they eat, and in their social habits. Non-Christians make fun of our "Christian Tamil," or whatever the Indian language is that we speak. Moreover, we don't go to the marriages or funerals of our Hindu or Muslim neighbors, nor are they invited to ours. In fact, we rarely mingle with them socially. True, there was a time when caste barriers prevented this. But now things are changing, and changing rapidly.

Cultural change in India is also bringing about social change. In their struggle for the recovery and reinterpretation of traditional cultural values and institutions, our countrymen are inspired by motives that are commendable and deserving of support. They are trying to safeguard the worth and dignity of the human person, to realize a true sense of human community, and to establish justice in human relations at all levels of society. As a religious minority, we Christians have a contribution to make to this double process of cultural disintegration and reintegration.

The second issue confronting Southern Asian Christians relates to forms of Christian worship, types of ministry and church organization, and the patterns of theological expression. What was handed down by our missionary fathers, we have only too carefully preserved. But do these forms and symbols, words and phrases, make sense, convey meaning, strike home? They are indeed valuable only insofar as they adequately represent the content of the faith that we seek to communicate.

The posture of devotion, the music to which our

hymns are set, the language we employ in prayer, in preaching, and in expounding Christian doctrines need to be adapted in each country to accord with the religious tradition of that land and its people. This is no new discovery. From the earliest days of Christianity's expansion, the need for such adaptation was recognized, although the process came to be arrested in the confusing age of European colonialism. During this long stretch of time, Christian people came to take it for granted that Christianity was best expressed only in Western forms. Now this assumption is open to question.

We Asian Christians ask, for instance, if the hymns we sing should only be translations in our various languages of what was originally written in English or German, and should they be sung only to Western music? The danger in such imitation is that form becomes more important than content—means develop into ends in themselves. What is more, such imitation prevents our churches from adventuring into faith, courageously experimenting with forms, symbols, and institutions that are familiar to the people and that would convey Christian truth and experience more effectively. Yet only in indigenous forms of expression can we make our witness of faith meaningful and relevant to our countrymen.

The third issue facing us arises out of the resurgence of other faiths, Hinduism, Buddhism, and Islam, and of the phenomenal spread of secularism in our countries. Unbelief and other belief are not peculiar to our age. What is peculiar, however, is that both unbelief and other belief are now vital forces in shaping the living and thinking of modern Asian and African man. And the believer, especially the Christian, has to reckon with them—not as systems of thought, but as living faiths that inspire the day-to-day conduct of leading men and women of our generation.

Although not fully worked out, there is profound insight in the traditional Hindu understanding of religion as being fourfold, *caturvarga.* These four ends of man are held to consist of righteous living, *dharma;* utilization of material wealth for spiritual ends, *artha;* all around development of the human person, *kāma;* and deliverance from the present to the ultimate state of being, or *moksha.* Contemporary trends in the renascence of religions in our world would seem to indicate that, however much we may differ as men of faith on our various understanding of deliverance (*moksha*), we are all endeavoring to realize similar ends in the areas of *dharma*, *artha*, and *kāma.* Are these, then, areas of religious cooperation in which we should be engaged, while zealously safeguarding the particularity of the Christian message of the gospel of the kingdom, which is the Christian view of *moksha?*

Christians are called to enter into a dialogue with

men of other faiths for yet another reason. Only through dialogue can they penetrate with sympathetic understanding the real significance of the "newness" present in contemporary Hinduism, Buddhism, and Islam. Can Christian faith discern in such renewal the inner working of the Spirit of God, guiding men of other faiths as well as men of no faith into a new understanding of God's ways with the world of men today? If all "new creation" can only be of God, where else could these new aspects of other beliefs have sprung from? If the whole creation is being directed toward the final "hope of glory" by the redemptive act of God in Jesus Christ, is fulfillment in the end the result of the present being fulfilled in the future? Or does it consist in the ultimate future being realized, and so fulfilled, in the temporal present? If the true reading of salvation history is in terms of Eternity flowing into Time, the coming of the Eternal Kingdom of God in the temporal order of man, how do we restate the distinctiveness of the gospel in the context of the religions of the world?

Such heart-searching questions will have to be faced by all Christians in this generation. These questions have no ready answer, and it is possible that all may not agree on any *one* answer. In any case, to find the answers, Christians need to know much more than they do now of the living faiths of other men, and, even more, of faiths whereby they themselves live. Somebody has said,

"The Christian community is at the moment theologically unequipped for living in the twentieth century, with its pluralistic mankind." That is so. Any ecumenical approach to contemporary concerns of Christian living and thinking will have to take account not only of diversity of denominations and of the new distinction between the younger and the older churches, but also of the cultural, national, and religious diversities in the world.

CHAPTER 4

Resurgent Religions: Faith and Nationhood

THE religions of Southern Asia are living realities, faiths whereby men live in the here and now. And yet it is only in recent times that Christians have come to accept their vitality. When modern missions began at the dawn of the eighteenth century, it looked as though Hinduism, Buddhism, and Islam were all losing ground. This was because Western knowledge of these religions was based on an imperfect study of their sacred books. Westerners had yet to learn the language in which each body of scriptures was written, and, in the case of Hinduism and Buddhism, the sacred literature was confusingly voluminous. Most knowledge was derived from the popular practices and beliefs that prevailed at the time. The gross idolatry of the Hindu, the vain asceticism of the Buddhist, the fanatic claims of the Muslim for the Prophet were easily recognized and were singled out for attack, since they were the indications of ignorance and folly. The early missionaries sincerely believed that such superstitious faiths should be totally destroyed. Only as Christians gained better understanding of the teachings of other religions, and came to know more intimately their devout adherents, did they realize the strength of these faiths.

REASONS FOR RESURGENCE

Today in Southern Asia, Hinduism, Islam, and Buddhism have a new lease on life. They are resurgent faiths for several reasons. One, of course, is nationalism. Independence seemed to imply not only the rejection of foreign rule but also all other foreign influence, especially in the realm of faith. There was an upsurge of pride in ancestral religions. In Pakistan this religious revival is the avowed policy of the state. In Ceylon the Sinhalese majority declares that Buddhism should be revived and restated. India, on the other hand, considers herself a secular state, but because of the fact that an overwhelming majority of the population is Hindu, Hinduism is a decisive factor in national life.

Another reason for this resurgence is the close tie between religion and cultural and social life. Islamic law is based on the Koran. The Hindu social code is derived from the *Dharma Sastras*, science of righteousness. The individual and social conduct of devout Sinhalese is directed by the Buddhist monks. But just as national cultural values have been restated to suit the modern age, religious beliefs and practices have also been revised. The resurgence of Asian religions is not a simple harking back to old beliefs and practices. It is a reinterpretation of sacred texts in a meaningful way for modern man and in terms of new learning and new insights.

One of the new emphases in these old faiths is upon the necessity of a religion giving men and women believers an enthusiasm for life in the present, for making the most of life's opportunities. All human effort to improve the lot of man is to be considered worthwhile. Thus in Hinduism and Buddhism, for instance, the teaching that what happens to a man in this life is determined by his previous life is restated to imply that how a man lives in this life will largely determine his next life. People should not pity themselves for what they are now; instead they should set about doing things that may improve their next life.

Another new emphasis is placed on man as a member

of a group. The purely individualistic understanding of salvation as something for which each man works on his own and for himself is now changing. Hindu *moksha,* or deliverance, is not to be considered as merely individual release. It is now being given a social meaning, though what is implied is not yet clearly stated. In Gāndhi's thinking, as it is now being explained by Vinoba Bhave, the goal in life is the welfare of all. The good of any man is achieved only insofar as the good of all is secured. Likewise, the good of all is possible only when the good of each man is guaranteed. In Buddhism the teaching concerning compassion is restated to mean social righteousness. Even the Muslim concept of jihad, or holy war, is set forth in terms that convey the idea of warring against all evil that is abhorrent to God. Social evil is considered such an evil by many contemporary Islamic writers.

A third new emphasis of the major faiths is on the acceptance of the material things of this world because they contribute to the welfare of man. The Hindu and Buddhist concept that matter is evil is no longer held in the same old way, consequently there is no longer the tendency to withdraw from the world. Hinduism and Buddhism both now recognize the value of the disciplined use of material goods for the enrichment of the human person. Underlying all the five-year-plans for national development in India is the passionate conviction that man in India, as Prime Minister Nehru once put it, will be a different person as a result of this national effort. A similar conviction is behind all the vast schemes for large scale industrial development in Pakistan, Ceylon, and Nepal.

Much of what is new in Asian religion derives from the Christian faith. These emphases are the result of thoughtful non-Christians having been deeply influenced in their own lives by Christian teachings. The Christian impact began in the very early days of Christian missions. The regeneration of Hinduism began with Rāmmohun Roy (1772–1833), who was a contemporary of William Carey and Alexander Duff in Calcutta. In Islam the early pioneer of reform was Sir Syed Ahmad Khan (1817–1898), who pleaded for modernization of Islam and the recognition of reason in interpreting koranic revelation.

At the risk of oversimplification, the renascence in Asian religions arising from encounter with Christianity may be said to have passed through three distinct phases. The first was the candid acceptance of certain Christian teachings. Hinduism and Buddhism adopted many Christian ideas, such as the worth and dignity of the human person, the value of corporate worship, and the reality of God's purposeful activity in human history. This early period was one of admiration for Christian truths and imitation of Christian ethics.

Not that Christianity as such was accepted, but some Christian beliefs and practices were adopted.

The next phase was one of reaction. Religious leaders began to fear that their traditional religions were being neglected. Reform was good, but it should not lead to uncritical denunciation of the ancestral faiths. In defense of the old, the new had to be reassessed. Revivalists arose and declared that what was being acclaimed as new in Christianity had been there all the time in the old faiths. Swāmī Vivekānanda (1863–1902) held such a position. He preached that what modern Hindu man found valuable in Christianity really was embodied in some of the earliest Hindu writings. Thus admiration and imitation gave place to criticism and rejection.

A third phase followed that accepted both reform and revival. Exponents of this approach held that the ancient faiths of Southern Asia should restate their traditional teachings in terms of the new insights. Christian truths and practices should be absorbed and made living components of the faith. The Hindu doctrine of the world as illusion, for instance, should be restated to affirm the reality of the world as created by God. In Islam, to cite another instance, a more comprehensive proscription was given to idol worship, extending Muhammad's teaching beyond idols of wood and stone to include any object of worship that misappropriated the honor and sovereignty due only to Almighty God.

RESURGENCE — THE HINDU EXAMPLE

All that has been said in a general way about the resurgence of Asian religions perhaps may be made more meaningful by taking a fuller view of renascent Hinduism in India. It should be remembered that eight out of every ten people in India are Hindu, and in the case of the ninth person, the chances of his also being a Hindu are fifty-fifty.

Hinduism is a vast complex of varying forms of worship and diverse doctrines. It has a voluminous body of scriptures that support different views about the nature of God and of his relation to the world of men. The Vedas (the most ancient of the Hindu scriptures) and the Upanishads (speculative treatises on the Vedas), on which are based the later Sutras (textbooks) of classical Hindu philosophy, give authority for the belief that God, as the Absolute Self, is apprehended in mystic realization of unity by the real self in man. On the other hand, the great epics, Mahābhārata and Rāmayāna, and the Purānas (legends) teach that God manifests himself to men in many forms, mainly as Vishnu and as Siva, and is to be worshiped in loving adoration. This form of Hinduism is more widespread among common folk than the philosophic religion of the Upanishads. The two sects of Vaishnavism and Saivism have developed their own separate bodies of sacred literature, their

74

different deities who are regarded as one or another of the many forms of Vishnu and Siva, their own symbolic expressions in worship, and their specific doctrines.

Quite early in Hindu religious consciousness the idea gained firm hold that a man's present life is but one of many, connected in unbroken sequence. This doctrine of *samsāra*, transmigration, carries with it the idea that the consequences of one's actions (karma) are carried over from life to life. The basic religious question to the Hindu is this: How can I find release from bondage to *karma-samsāra?*

Religious thought in Hinduism has been concerned with: the nature of karma and its relation to the human agent; the distinction between the actual doer, which is the human person, and the real "I," which is the soul or true self; and lastly, the realm of eternal being, where there is no activity and, therefore, no *karma-samsāra*.

Hindu religious devotion, on the other hand, has developed a traditional literature in the vernacular as distinguished from the philosophical writings in the classical Sanskrit. These books describe (1) the concern of Siva and Vishnu for the devotee and their gracious willingness to help him to secure deliverance; (2) the ecstatic adoration and loving devotion of the devotee to the object of worship; and (3) the ultimate state of beatitude when the devotee, released from this-worldly existence, abides in fellowship with the Divine.

Hindu religious observances, consisting mainly of traditional rites, have multiplied as believers have sought to accumulate merit so that the evil consequences of their actions might be counteracted. The more a person frequents the temple and goes on pilgrimage to sacred shrines, and the more faithful he is in observing prescribed rites at birth, marriage, and death, the greater the sum of merit to his credit.

Such religious activities, sometimes known as Popular Hinduism, have grown since Indian independence. Many Hindu state officials make it a point to visit the more important temples and pilgrimage centers on their official tours, and this has given new significance to these shrines for the common folk. It is also becoming accepted practice to open public functions with an invocation that is Hindu in form and content. Another innovation is group singing of Hindu sacred songs not only because of a revived interest in classical music but also to promote a spirit of devotion. A great deal of the radio and cinema music in India deals with religious themes from traditional literature.

In rural areas, especially among what were formerly outcaste and low-caste groups, the worship of village goddesses is common. Such local deities are believed to protect the village from disease, drought, and disaster. Formerly, when calamity overtook a village, the whole village used to offer sacrifices of goats and buffaloes to placate the goddesses whose anger was presumed to have caused the trouble. Such gruesome rites are now being stopped by state action. But belief in goddesses is still prevalent in rural India. The country people feel that for the everyday needs of life, for success in daily work, for the blessing of children, for the cure of some persistent disease these deities are more readily persuaded to help than others. The shrines raised to them are usually rude structures along a wayside, unlike the elaborate temples of traditional Hindu gods and goddesses. People of all sorts—educated high-caste folk and illiterate laborers, sometimes Muslims and Christians —make their vows at the shrines, promising to offer a sacrifice if a particular boon is granted.

The wide variety of Hindu beliefs and practices is reconciled by the doctrine that all ways lead to the same goal. This tolerance of Hinduism, its spirit of accommodation to different doctrines and observances, is based on the conviction that the essential nature of the Ultimate Reality is unknowable. It can only be partially apprehended in human existence. Therefore, no claims for absolute truth can be made by any religious community. On the other hand, it is believed that men of faith should be willing to accede that there is both truth and falsity in all religions. Since such conditions prevail, people should be let alone to work out their own creed, as individuals and as groups, according to their own light. Today Hinduism claims to be not one religion but a comprehensive and all inclusive family of religions described by the term *Sanātana Dharma*, Eternal Dharma —a beginningless and endless religion that stretches over the whole span of time and includes the entire concourse of humanity.

Since the beginning of the nineteenth century, Hinduism has become increasingly conscious of a surge of new life that is due to national awakening in India and encounter with the modern world. The main emphases in resurgent Hinduism are upon reform of social evils associated with traditional Hinduism, restatement of certain beliefs that have become antiquated, and revival of certain other beliefs in order that Hinduism may make a vital contribution to world religious thought. Thoughtful Hindus have frequently realized that there were unwholesome social practices in Hinduism that needed reform. Rāmmohun Roy, whose indebtedness to Christianity we have already noted, was the earliest of these reformers. He drew pointed attention to the inhuman traditions that made the lot of Hindu women intolerable. In his day the practice of burning the widow on the funeral pyre of her dead husband was widely observed. Child marriage was common, and many a girl whose marriage was never consummated was condemned to live a miserably neglected life if her husband died prematurely. Widow remarriage was unthinkable.

Girls could not go to school or learn a trade, much less enter a profession. In short, women had no rights.

The movement that Rāmmohun Roy founded was no mere agitation for the recognition of the equality of women. For the first time in the history of Hinduism, the issue of the dignity of the human person was raised. It is no wonder that concern for discrimination against women widened to include the larger problem of discrimination in all of Hindu society, notably that resulting from the caste system. The Hindu reformers of nineteenth century India were influenced, on one hand, by the Christian teaching of the missionary colleges they had attended, and on the other, by the Western liberalism that marked the new system of education being introduced by the British. Rāmmohun Roy was not only well versed in the Christian scriptures; he was profoundly influenced by Western liberalism.

As the nineteenth century advanced, nationalism gathered force, and the struggle for freedom from foreign domination took form and content. With it developed the new emphasis on the dignity of the human person. The immediate need for breaking down divisions in Hindu society based on the caste structure absorbed all attention. Even before Mahatma Gāndhi appeared on the scene, the pernicious practice of "untouchability" was singled out for attack. But it was left to Gāndhi to lead the crusade against this evil and to throw open the temples to the outcastes. Today, no longer outcastes, the former "untouchables" are known by the name given them by Gāndhi—*harijan*, the people of God. The worth of the human person established by reason of God's concern in man!

Since Indian independence, all discriminations based on caste and sex have been legally abolished. The modern concept of human rights has been generally accepted and upheld by law. Considerable social legislation has been put into effect, the most comprehensive and radical being the Hindu Code Bill. But the fact remains that traditional ideas about the place of women and "the caste spirit" are still embarrassingly prevalent. What is lacking is the religious conviction that the worth and dignity of the human person are guaranteed by the supreme fact of the Divine Person, and that true human community involves the belief that he is verily at the center of it, providing the one dynamic bond of association.

Closely allied with the concept of human worth is that of social justice. "The fear of Christianity was the beginning of social wisdom in Hinduism," observed a Hindu social reformer recently. That is putting it negatively. Hindu involvement in movements for social justice did begin as a defense reaction, but it also developed out of the recognition that Hindu ethics needed improvement. Traditional Hindu ethics are primarily individual, pietistic, and legalistic. The network of human relations that make society a community was never visualized. Thus the caste structure tended toward fragmentation and separation of caste and sub-caste, instead of fusing them into a larger, interdependent community. Caste in India had tended to safeguard group interests and to promote the welfare of one group at the expense of other groups. It represented a kind of group selfishness.

The evil of religious and caste communalism became apparent in the days of the national struggle for independence. It was one factor that quickened Hindu sensitivity to social injustice. Another factor was the new industrial economy that came to be widely accepted. A third, but by no means the least, was the impact of Christian teaching about man in society. Not that Christianity had helped realize the ideal of a responsible society, but the fact that it had repeatedly expressed contrition because of its tragic failure to uphold the ideal—this was the challenge to Hindu leaders.

John Ruskin's *Unto this Last* was the immediate source of inspiration for Gāndhi's *sarvodaya* ideal of "the welfare of all." During Gāndhi's own lifetime this ideal provided the social philosophy underlying plans for Indian basic education. After his death it furnished the dynamic for the *bhūdān*, land-gift, movement of Vinobā Bhāve and the *gram raj* program of Jai Prakash Narayan, which emphasized social ethics and social discipline. More recently, the Indian government has sponsored a program of village community development directed toward achieving social justice in Indian life.

No less significant has been the increasing interest in social service. Here again the reasons are many and complex. But surely the concept of service (*seva*) is not fundamentally Hindu. The term, "missionary zeal," which is often used in commending *seva* to volunteers, is a tacit admission of at least one non-Hindu source of inspiration. There is no doubt that Swāmī Vivekānanda modeled the service program of the Rāmakrishna Mission on that of the Christian missions of his day. Orphanages, schools, hospitals, dispensaries, and emergency relief work in famine stricken or flood destroyed areas were the usual forms in which Hindu *seva* was given expression. Gopāl Krishna Gokhale as early as 1905 established the Servants of India Society. The society sought to enlist young Hindu intellectuals in a lifetime of disciplined service. During the period of the nationalist struggle, and since independence, innumerable *seva ashrams* have sprung up all over the country, inculcating hundreds of young Hindus with the concept of service.

It was Swāmī Vivekānanda, again, who spelled out the Hindu religious justification for social service. He said that it expressed, in this world of seeming differences, the transcendental truth of an ultimate Oneness.

What is done to another, then, is done to one's own self, since all being is, in the final count, but the Ultimate Self.

Beyond the interest in social justice and social service, the idea has gained ground that the highest end in life is not total withdrawal from activity but purposeful endeavor to achieve the common good. In a sense, this emphasis on action is a reaction against a common over-statement that Hindus are fatalists and world-and-life-denying mystics. The whole surge toward nationhood comprehends this enlarged Hindu understanding. The various five-year-plans of the Indian government have been developed on the assumption that definite objectives are reached by working for them.

Modern India owes this new understanding to Bāl Gangādhar Tilak (1856–1920) more than to any other nationalist leader. In his commentary on the *Gītā*,[1] Tilak forcefully showed that action was fundamental to the understanding of karma. More recent commentators have taken a similar stand. The cyclical interpretation of history in modern Hindu thought has resulted in a point of view such as that expressed by Radha Kamal Mukerji that "history is essentially the chronicle of *nārā* [man] becoming *nārottama* [perfect man] and finally merging into *Nārāyana* [God]." This is similar to what Sarvepalli Radhakrishnan holds. "The meaning of

[1] The *Bhagavad Gītā, Song of the Lord*, is the best known of all Hindu writings and forms a part of the great epic of India, the *Mahābhārata*.

history," for Radhakrishnan, "is to make all men prophets to establish a kingdom of free spirits. The infinitely rich and impregnated future, this drama of the gradual transmutation of intellect into spirit, of son of man into son of God, is the goal of history. When death is overcome, when time is conquered, the kingdom of the eternal spirit is established."

FAITH AND SOCIETY

The religious situation in India today is the outcome of the interaction between two forces, religious orthodoxy and modern life. On one hand, religious leaders have been compelled to justify the claims of traditional religion as being still meaningful. On the other, the pressure of far-reaching changes in social attitudes and traditional mores have called for the restatement of long accepted beliefs. The resurgence of Hinduism demonstrates both its vitality and its capacity for adaptation. It provides its followers with a dynamic faith that supports their efforts to improve human welfare. It undergirds the remodeling of the social structure and human relations so that the dignity of the person is safeguarded. Hinduism has become alive in a new way to assert its claims as the living faith of more than 85 per cent of the population in New India.

Since independence, the people of India have sought to strengthen their sense of selfhood, their consciousness of themselves as a people among other people in the world. The natural tendency among Southern Asians is to build such feeling of national coherence and solidarity on the bedrock of a common faith. Generally, Indians regard Hinduism as this faith. In addition, a growing vocal and militant minority would go further and make Hinduism the state religion. Extremists hold that only those who profess Hinduism can claim full citizenship rights. However, the manifest intention of the leaders who drafted the constitution of the Indian Republic was to set up a secular state. Mahatma Gāndhi was insistent upon this and the present government under Nehru's leadership is anxious that the secular ideal should eventually be realized. This does not mean that the state recognizes no religion but rather that it gives equal regard to all religions. Further, no discrimination is to be made on account of religious beliefs, the constitution stating very clearly that all citizens shall have freedom "to profess, practise, and propagate religion."

The fact that Indians have accepted a parliamentary form of government is another factor in the situation. Every citizen has the right to vote for his representative in the various state legislatures as well as the central legislature. But demagogues seeking election often play up religious and caste prejudices, and some political parties have also been guilty of this misconduct. Religious communalism, the most sinister single force endangering national unity in the days of the British regime, is rearing its head again. Religious minorities are beginning to fear that the Hindu majority is dominating the national scene and is resorting to political expedients to safeguard and enhance its own interests. The situation is further complicated by the close connection between Hindu cultural values and institutions and Hindu religious ideas and practices. To religious minorities, the cultural renaissance following independence has sometimes given the impression that it is all a subtle process of Hinduization.

There recently have been ugly manifestations of Hindu extremism with violent suppressions of minority rights. Protests by religious minorities like the Sikhs in the Punjab, the Muslims in Madhya Pradesh, and the Christian tribes in Assam are mounting, and the Indian government has found it necessary to take steps to counter the spread of religious fanaticism, which is deplored both on moral grounds and as a threat to unity.

As we have already seen, Indian nationalist leaders early realized that certain social evils like untouchability, hereditary caste restrictions, and the suppression of women needed radical treatment if India were to realize a true sense of nationhood. Many of these pernicious customs were traditionally sanctioned by religion. Although the British were averse to interfering with the religious prejudices of the people, several reforms were put into effect during their rule. Since independence, the Indian government has boldly introduced reform measures, arousing orthodox and conservative Hindus in the process. The Hindu Code Bill and the recently enacted Dowry Bill are but two such pieces of social legislation that have brought about truly revolutionary changes in the social and political status of Hindu women. Another far-reaching enactment is the legal abolition of untouchability and of all caste discrimination in regard to citizenship rights.

But such laws, however helpful, have not wiped out caste attitudes that supersede legislative action and actually nullify the intended good. Indeed, the reactionary forces of Hindu religious orthodoxy have proved serious deterrents to national progress and social change. However, there is a large liberal group in Hinduism that actively sympathizes with the movement for social reform and holds it to be in accord with the spirit of Hindu fundamentals.

A significant minority in India would press for more drastic social and economic change, even if this involves repudiation of religious beliefs. This minority may be said to fall into three groups. One group, of outcaste origin, in western and central India owes its inspiration to the great *harijan* leader, B. R. Ambedkar. This group actually left the Hindu fold in protest and adopted a form of Buddhism that adheres to the ethical and humanistic teachings of the Buddha.

A second group, mostly confined to the south, militantly opposes traditional Hinduism, denouncing it as a deliberate device of the priestly Brahman caste to keep the other castes under ignorant subjection and social servitude. This group's own religious position has not been in any sense defined, but members hold in reverence the humanistic teachings of Buddha and those of an ancient Tamil sage, Tiruvalluvar, whose great work, the *Kural*, is their Bible. The rationalistic attacks on religion by Robert Ingersoll, the well-known American agnostic, seem to have a special appeal to them and they have translated many of his essays into Tamil.

The third group consists of radical socialists, some of whom are members of the Communist party of India. Religion, including Hinduism, is regarded as deadening to the social conscience and the intellectual integrity of all peoples. At best this group is indifferent to religion, and an extreme wing would describe itself as openly atheistic.

Modern science and technology have stirred diverse reactions among Hindu intellectuals. There was a time when the more orthodox and conservative Hindu leaders denounced industrialization as evidence of a Western materialism that was opposed to Eastern spirituality. Now the general tendency is to accept material goods as contributing to the welfare of man in the here and now. There is a recognition of the worthiness of human existence and the meaningfulness of present history.

The rapid industrialization of the country has produced a new class of factory workers who are mostly of low-caste origin. Many among them have given up traditional customs and institutions, but that does not mean that they have ceased to profess Hinduism, much less that they have turned away from all religion. Wherever labor colonies are established, Hindu worship places are also invariably built. It is not uncommon in the larger factories for workers to worship together at times of official gatherings and Hindu festivals. The idea is firmly rooted in the Hindu mind that earthly prosperity is the gift of the gods; to win their favor (and avoid their displeasure) periodic offerings must be made to them. Labor unions may successfully resist exploitation and injustice, but the good things of life are benefits from the gods. It is not a coincidence that in almost every place where new industrial projects or river valley schemes have developed, new places of Hindu worship also have been built.

The urbanization that has come in the wake of industrialization has by no means weakened the hold of religion on the masses, though it has made them sensitive to the violation of human rights and to all social injustice. In industrial areas the iniquity of caste discrimination is felt keenly. This has given rise to vigorous demands that the social structure of Hindu India be repatterned without reference to traditional religious sanctions.

Secularization of society is a long-term process, and India is now only witnessing its beginning. At this stage, the trend is unrelated to the prevailing Hindu concept of the sacred. Consequently, the new social philosophy is developing side by side with, but in no way related to, the basic beliefs of popular Hinduism as expressed in temple worship, pilgrimages, and domestic rites. With the awakening of the ordinary man, the factory laborer and the peasant, resurgent Hinduism will have to face the problem of showing how everyday religion, as opposed to the philosophy of the classical scholar, can furnish an adequate spiritual basis for life in the New India.

NEW CHALLENGE TO CHRISTIANS

Christians are also called to rethink their affirmations of faith. The basis of Christian faith is in the biblical revelation. The testimony of the Bible is clear: that God is the creator of all men, that his salvation in Jesus Christ is offered to all men, and that in him there is a new creation. Jesus Christ is the way and the truth and the life (John 14:6). In him God's promise to his people was fulfilled, and through his cross and his glorious resurrection all men of all nations have "access in one Spirit to the Father" (Eph. 2:18). Christians are called to be the community of witness to his salvation and his kingdom. Through the religious and secular movements of our time, God is leading mankind to perceive the true meaning of the new creation in Jesus Christ.

Christians are by no means worthy of this mission to witness. Nor have they always been faithful. Religious men of other faiths, judged by the standards of their religions, are frequently more religious than we are as Christians. It has been said that: "Neither in the strength of religious consciousness nor in the depths of metaphysical thinking, neither in the awareness of harmony with the universe nor in the effort for spiritual self-liberation can we claim as Christians to excel those who are not Christians." That is so. But we are called to be obedient to the missionary mandate of our Lord. We are called to proclaim in all humility the uniqueness of God's revelation in the Lord Jesus Christ, "For the word of the cross is folly to those who are perishing, but to us who are being saved it is the power of God" (I Cor. 1:18).

This pressing demand to proclaim the Word of God forced itself on the attention of the Christian church in Southern Asia at the famous missionary gathering, in 1938, at Madras. Since then, the tendency has been to emphasize the revelation aspect of the gospel as completely different from, and discontinuous with, other religions. This theological approach was a needed corrective, but it did make it difficult if not impossible for Christians to enter into fruitful conversation with men of other faiths. Today, it is recognized that without such confrontation with other faiths, Christian witness cannot be arrestingly relevant and meaningful. Especially in the present situation in Asia, economic and social change is creating unprecedented pressures on the people.

Asian conditions have changed beyond all recognition since the Madras meeting. The change gives a new urgency to Christian witness. Modern Asian man is concerned with revolutionary plans for the remaking of society, for the realization of personal values, and the achievement of specific national goals. He is searching for spiritual foundations for this new world, and he does not always find the needed dynamic of faith in the traditional religion of his fathers. Modern religious movements in the historic religions of Asia stand for two things. On the one hand, there are indications of the crises brought about by the inadequacy of traditional institutions and theological beliefs. On the other hand, there are efforts to recover the support of faith by a radical renewal of belief in terms of present day demands and needs. Religion and society in Asian lands are closely interrelated. The gospel of Jesus Christ has to be proclaimed as the good news of the God who is concerned with man in his relations to other men, and to the world of things.

A world renewed in Christ, the new creation, is the sum and substance of the message of the Christian witness. It is the high calling of the fellowship of the Christian church to be the pledge of this new creation. At this point, Christians come up against the central issue raised by renascent non-Christian religions: Is the preaching of the gospel directed to the total annihilation of all other religions? Will religions as religions, and nations as nations, continue characteristically separate in the fullness of time when God will ". . . unite all things in him, things in heaven and things on earth" (Eph. 1:10)?

Christians believe in the final gathering up of all that is of this world and of the next in the resurrection life, but it is not for us to indicate what will be preserved, and in what manner. We cannot tell how God will bring his purpose for mankind and his world to a conclusion. But insofar as Christians identify themselves with the will of God as revealed in Christ, they can be certain that they will be working along the line of that purpose and not against it.

Christian faith distinguishes between the gospel proclamation of the fulfillment of God's promise of the kingdom, and the hope in fulfillment of all religious faith, wherever it is found. Fulfillment in the second sense would mean that all sincere human striving to reach out to God will find favor with him. The history of religions is based on this hope. There well may be a more or less progressive development in the history of man's understanding about God. It can be traced back to the primitive past, discerned in the living present, and perfected at the end in the future. But fulfillment in the distinctly Christian sense means that, because the promise of the kingdom is so totally assured, the end is in reality a present fact. It is come! In salvation-history, to the discerning eye of faith, the eternal future is being fulfilled in the contemporary present. It is in this sense that our Lord declared that he had come not to destroy but to fulfill.

This is the scandal in the foolishness of Christian witness to Jesus Christ as revealing the timeless and eternal God. This claim we may not be able to substantiate by reasoning alone. It can only be commended by faith to faith, for ". . . no one can say 'Jesus is Lord' except by the Holy Spirit" (1 Cor. 12:3). This is not a mere matter of propagandizing others or of seeking to dominate their thinking by overwhelming pressure, whether political, social, or economic. It is rather a question of obedience to the Lordship of Jesus Christ in one's own life. It is bearing witness to the faithfulness of God that a man has encountered in Christ, and demanding of that man a corresponding fidelity to God. And that demand is a call that enlightens and rouses to action. It carries with it mission, beside which there can be no other mission. "Ye are my witnesses!" "Go ye into all the world!" "And this gospel of the kingdom will be preached throughout the whole world, as a testimony to all nations; and then the end will come" (Matt. 24:14).

C H A P T E R *5*

Growing in Unity

SOUTHERN Asian Christians have had no choice in the matter of denominational loyalties. They are the children of various missions. When they became Christians, they accepted without question the denominational pattern of their missionary fathers. In fact, in the early days, these Asian Christians described themselves as London Mission Christians, American Arcot Mission Christians, and so forth. To them, denominational distinctions were almost meaningless. If they meant anything at all, it was in terms of geography. If Methodists worked in a certain part of the country, Christians there became Methodists. It was as simple as that. They might have been Presbyterians if the area had been evangelized by Presbyterians. As a matter of fact, when people migrated from one place to another and found there a church of another denomination, they became members of that church. A Congregationalist, for instance, could become an Anglican overnight in this way. Moreover, from the very beginning, Asian Christians married across denominational lines, and it is not uncommon for the members of a Christian family to have diverse denominational backgrounds.

THE RISE OF DENOMINATIONALISM

Denominational loyalty did develop at a later stage, but it was not always due to an understanding of theological differences. It must be stated, though, that where denominational indoctrination was done with some thoroughness, especially among second and third generations, people have sincere convictions as Anglicans, Lutherans, or Methodists. This is true in Ceylon among many Sinhalese Anglicans and Methodists. By and large, however, other factors have entered into the rise of denominationalism. Frequently, employment in a denominational institution developed such loyalty, though it has not always been clear whether the loyalty was to the denomination, the institution, or to the missionary employer. Sometimes denominational loyalties got mixed up with caste loyalties. In one part of India, for instance, American Baptist work produced converts primarily from one outcaste group. American Lutherans started their mission work in a neighboring area, drawing their converts from another low-caste group. Today the distinction between these two denominations is made on the basis of caste origin rather than on anything else. The difference has been heightened by the fact that these two different caste groups do not intermarry.

The confusion created by denominationalism has been a great hindrance to evangelism. This was certainly realized early enough. Even in the nineteenth century, it became necessary to come to some understanding about dividing the proliferating areas of work so that possible conflict and unseemly rivalry could be avoided. Comity arrangements were, therefore, devised quite early in missionary history. According to this system it was agreed that Protestant missions should limit their evangelistic work to carefully defined geographical areas. Such an arrangement was a sort of gentlemen's agreement to prevent poaching on each other's preserves. It worked well until it was realized that comity only perpetuated denominationalism. What is more, it resulted in regionalism. Missionaries themselves realized the awkwardness of such agreements, especially in view of the evangelistic task to witness. What really pricked was the question whether people of other faiths should become Christians—or Baptists, Anglicans, Congregationalists, and so forth. Moreover, it became increasingly apparent that wastage in men and money could be avoided if denominational forces were persuaded to co-operate; this would certainly make for more effective witness, too, especially in service projects.

From comity to co-operation was the next step that missions took in Asian lands, beginning early in the twentieth century. Not that denominational differences were denied, but, accepting the fact of denominations, plans were made to join forces by pooling resources in men and money, especially in the fields of education and medical work. One significant area in which interdenominational co-operation was introduced was the training of candidates for the ministry. In India three outstanding theological colleges have developed in consequence, one in Serampore, another in Bangalore, and more recently a third in Jabalpur. Although these schools were established in India, they helped to train the ministry for churches in India, Pakistan, and Ceylon. Apart from the fact that theological training has been upgraded through such co-operation, the future ministers of the various churches in neighboring lands were brought together, and better understanding was created among both faculty and students. Co-operation in theological training has paid large dividends in terms of Christian unity.

A strengthened unity cannot be claimed for co-operative institutions engaged in other educational work or in medicine, however. It is true that from the standpoint of professional standards, and efficiency as welfare agencies, these institutions are absolutely first-rate. But because denominational biases are still preserved, and in some cases in an exaggerated form, they are unable to give a unity of witness. As professional institutions, they function together, it is true, but as evangelistic agencies, they still prefer to retain their separatist propaganda.

STEPS TOWARD UNITY

Asian Christians, themselves, are not interested in either comity or co-operation. After all, these are strategic measures for the smooth and efficient working of missions *as missions*. They have little meaning for churches as churches. Churches are not "contained" by comity agreements. Churches function as one, not together. From the standpoint of the life of the churches, co-operation is only a halfway measure, a compromise, not a full-blooded expression of vitality. Consequently, when local Christian congregations outgrew their stage of dependence on missions, they set about planning for unity. It was realized that only a united church could present an effective witness in a non-Christian land.

Comity and co-operation do not eradicate the evil of denominationalism, they only tend to perpetuate these differences. Unity in evangelism calls for a united church that is conscious of its mission to proclaim the gospel.

In each of the countries of Southern Asia this concern for the organic unity of the church has grown by leaps and bounds. In India, even before the turn of the century, there were movements for church unity within denominational families. Some Presbyterian groups got together as early as 1875, and Lutheran missions were working unitedly in scattered areas a few years later. Attempts were made for several years to unite groups across denominational lines, finally culminating in the formation of the South India United Church in 1908. This union embraced bodies of Presbyterian, Reformed, and Congregational backgrounds. Presbyterians and Congregationalists in North India joined together on a federal basis and formed the United Church of Northern India some years later.

Such was the beginning of the unity movement. In time the question of union with other denominations was presented to the large Anglican church in South India. For them, in particular, to unite with churches of non-episcopal tradition, recognizing other ministries while preserving their traditional liturgical practices and continuing their relationship with their parent churches, presented serious difficulties. In South India these issues were squarely faced. Over a long period, consultations were held in which Presbyterians, Congregationalists, Methodists, and Anglicans took increasing interest. It was clear that only when the scandal of denominationalism was brought to an end could the missionary task of the church in India be fulfilled. Union was undoubtedly the will of God, and about that the teaching of the Scriptures was emphatic. But differences could not be resolved overnight.

As the discussions proceeded it was recognized that there were three chief difficulties. One was the fact that the historical episcopate traceable to New Testament times had to be approved by all the uniting churches. This meant that those who had not been used for centuries to the idea of episcopacy—the free churches, so-called—should agree to accept it. And they did.

The second problem concerned the difficulties that stood in the way of mutual recognition of the ministry, the sacrament of the Lord's Supper. In South India it was agreed that, for the sake of unity, the validity of the ministry of all churches should be accepted. For the first time in the history of the church the ministers of all churches, both those who had been episcopally ordained and those who had not been so ordained, were to be permitted to continue as ministers of the united church. After union, all those who were newly admitted into the ministry would be ordained by bishops. Thus it became possible that when the sacrament of the Lord's Supper was celebrated by any minister of the Church of South India, all members of that church could receive it.

The third difficulty was not so insuperable. Continued relation with the parent churches in the West, particularly in terms of missionary personnel and financial aid, could only be maintained on the understanding that the Church of South India was an autonomous church. This was cutting across the authority of denominational mission boards, but the uniting parties agreed. However, in the case of the Anglican communion, the concession had to be made with certain reservations.

The Church of South India came into existence in 1947. It was not so much of an achievement, really, as it was a beginning. We members cannot say that within the Church of South India all differences have been wiped out completely. But then our goal has been unity, not uniformity. We pride ourselves on our "comprehensiveness." We have taken the courageous step of preserving all the values of our diverse heritage and this contributes to the richness and variety of our worship and congregational life. But the process of integration is still going on. So also is the continued effort to bring into the union other churches in South India who are not yet a part. There is, for example, the big Lutheran church that is spread over all the Tamil and the Telugu countries. There is again the Baptist group, which is largely concentrated in the Telugu area. Negotiations are underway more successfully with the Lutherans than with the Baptists.

In North India a similar movement for union has been under way, involving such diverse groups as the American Methodists and the British Baptists. A new feature of the North India scheme is the decision to make the ministry uniform at the outset. An act of commissioning will be administered to all ordained ministers in order that they may have added grace to serve the united church. The North India union plan, which would also apply to the churches in Pakistan, was considered, only a few months ago, to be in its final stages. However, since the various church councils began voting, early returns have shown sentiment running strongly against union. If this unexpected trend continues, it will be unfortunate indeed for the mission of the church. It would seem that, inevitably, the churches must reach some kind of an agreement, but considerable doubt now hangs over the whole project.

Similarly in Ceylon. One difficulty has arisen because of the relationship between nationality groups. Most of the Tamil Congregationalists in the northern part of Ceylon are already in the Diocese of Jaffna, which is part of the Church of South India. Their fellow Tamils who are Methodist have been very much influenced by this and lean toward union. On the other hand, the

Methodist Sinhalese show strong denominational loyalties, in part a reaction to the somewhat pronounced Catholic position of most Sinhalese Anglicans. What is really holding up progress is the different interpretation given to the official act of mutual commissioning of the ministry, a feature of the Ceylon scheme for union as of the North India plan.

THE ECUMENICAL MOVEMENT

The original impetus for the ecumenical movement in our time undoubtedly came from the sense of urgency emanating from mission lands, where a divided witness was defeating the church. But it is also true that the ecumenical movement, in its turn, has contributed a great deal toward promotion of plans for union. Chiefly, this has consisted in encouraging a deeper understanding of the biblical basis of the church, an appreciation of denominational heritage and tradition, especially in forms of worship, and a re-emphasis on the real nature of the mission of the church. All the movements toward union in India and Ceylon have been greatly influenced by the ecumenical studies in which member groups have been privileged to share. It may well be claimed that within the last twenty-five years the trend toward church union has not only been impelled by missionary enthusiasm but also strengthened by theological conviction.

WORLD CONFESSIONALISM

Alongside the ecumenical movement, and partly as a result of it, there has developed something of a countervailing force. This is represented in the growth of world confessional bodies, such as the Lutheran World Federation and the World Presbyterian Alliance. These are new phenomena, many coming into existence only since the second world war. Their express purpose is to create a sense of belonging and denominational pride on a world-wide scale. By educating their members on the distinctiveness of their doctrinal heritage, they try to foster a sense of close interdependence among regional denominational churches so that they are ready and willing to give one another needed assistance in personnel and finance. With this end in view, they produce considerable popular literature. Moreover, by periodically assembling for world-wide meetings, they are able to develop plans for mutual counseling and sharing, especially in matters relating to the mission of the church. In all these developments the United States seems to play a leading role, largely because of the abundant resources at her disposal.

What effect have these world confessional organizations on the movement for union in the churches of Southern Asia? Have they helped or hindered? Opinion is divided, but the majority view in India and in Ceylon is that they are a source of hindrance. The reasons are many. One is that denominations have now become conscious of their world dimension! There was a time when the Tamil Lutherans, for example, felt drawn to their parent Lutheran church in Denmark, Sweden, or Germany, as the case might be. Now they take pride in belonging to the Lutheran World Federation where they are made increasingly aware of their responsibilities with Lutherans the world over, while assistance in men and money now comes to them from Lutherans everywhere. This new sense of interdependence and mutual obligation is good in itself. But when it is narrowly tied up with denominational loyalties, it turns into something quite different. For instance, Tamil and Telugu Lutherans, aided by finances from their world confessional organization, are now doing missionary work in Indonesia. This is, of course, good, but in carrying on their task of witness they have become interested chiefly in promoting and strengthening denominational loyalties both in India and in Indonesia. The same holds true for Ceylon Methodists who have been aided in their mission work in Africa by their denominational world-wide agency.

Then again, the voluminous literature produced by world confessional bodies is specifically designed to bring out the characteristic differences in their denominational interpretations of Christian doctrine, the peculiar values in denominational forms of worship and hymnology, and the historical associations bound up with their particular tradition. Actually, much of this literature has little relation to the church in India, Pakistan, or Ceylon; it deals rather with the story of the origin and expansion of the denomination in the Old World amid conflicts and controversies that no longer make sense.

A couple of years ago a study was undertaken of selected local congregations in India, the backgrounds of which were British Anglican, American Methodist, and Swedish Lutheran. The survey revealed that the hold of denominational loyalties on these local congregations was noticeably on the increase. And yet in every case these congregations were connected with church councils involved in plans for union. Local leaders seemed to be more interested and informed about the world confessional body to which they belonged than about the current discussion on plans for union. To be still more specific, it was reported that, in the case of the Methodists, so many pastors had been visiting America one after another that the people in these congregations knew more about their denominational background than they did about the Indian church. Moreover, in one case a brand new American-modeled parish house, complete with dining halls and kitchen, was a constant reminder of the "parental" concern of

the church "back home." Would such gifts and priv-
ileges continue if these congregations became part of
the united church?

This is not to suggest that denominational loyalties
depend on subsidies. Nor does it imply that the generous
help given by parent churches from abroad is altogether
determined by denominational considerations. But it
does seem true that with the growth of world confessional
organizations, giving in the older churches, especially
for missions, tends to be bound by denominational considerations. This creates an unwholesome fear in the
younger churches that assistance from abroad may
steadily diminish and eventually stop, if denominational
connections cease. At the time of the inauguration of the
Church of South India, a group of Anglicans in the
Telugu area and another in the Tamil region stayed
out on this score.

There is yet another way in which world confessional
organization retards progress toward organic union.
Representatives of some national branches of these
world organizations seem to assume that they have a
vested interest in union plans, even when their country
made no missionary contribution to the churches involved in union. This was the situation, for instance,
when the Anglican dioceses in South India entered
into union negotiations. In the long drawn out process
of negotiation the matter took on the proportions of a

pan-Anglican issue. Church union in South India became a concern of Anglicans everywhere, and not all of them possessed an informed understanding. In America many members of the Protestant Episcopal Church felt that they had a say in the matter too, though at that time they had no missionary connection with South India.

An outstanding Presbyterian minister, who is deeply involved in the church union negotiations in North India, complained bitterly recently that this matter of periodically reporting to the respective world confessional bodies about the union scheme was very frustrating. Every member of each denominational body seemed to think that something needed to be said every time. Or as a Lutheran leader interested in joining the Church of South India put it: "How can we make Lutheran church leaders in Germany or Indonesia or America get to feel the situation in South India and experience the same urgency as we do about union, especially in the Lutheran World Federation where the matter has now to be talked out?" Is it any wonder that progress in union efforts is held up when these world bodies meet once in four years, and sometimes as infrequently as ten years?

In the case of institutions like hospitals, colleges, and theological seminaries, the tendency is to stop co-operation and put off development of union institutions now that subsidies come through world denominational bodies. One reason for this development is that what we in the younger churches call interdenominational ventures, meaning thereby co-operative institutions, now are invariably interpreted by the older churches in these world organizations as "ecumenical" and therefore "union" institutions! When we talk of co-operative institutions, we Asians mean undertakings by denominations as denominations in co-operation. They are not the same as union institutions that are maintained by the church without reference to denominational backgrounds. Another source of misunderstanding is that by the merging of institutional activities of different groups (missions) within the same denomination, "union" institutions have been brought into being. World confessionalism has been in some measure responsible for this development. The consequence is to strengthen denominationalism—not to help further the union of the churches! Lutherans working in India, for instance, have thought it wise to maintain a high grade theological college on an all-India Lutheran basis. And the Anglicans maintain a similar institution, although there is a possibility of their joining a united theological college of established standing and international reputation in their neighborhood. It is interesting to recall, in this connection, that before the birth of the Lutheran World Federation, the Tamil Lutherans were associated with such a united theological college in the Tamil country. The point is that the revival of denominationalism on a world-wide scale not only retards all progress towards church union but it tends to put a wrong construction on the very idea of the church. What is worse, it diverts attention from the trend toward organic union by setting up attractive immediate goals for ventures that are miscalled "union."

There is another question also. What consequence has world confessionalism on the cultural growth and national life of the Asian churches? Indigenization is not only a negative endeavor to rid the church of its foreignness, it is also a positive effort to make the church at home in its cultural environment. Discarding such foreign associations as music, architecture, church furnishing, and personnel do not by themselves make the church indigenous. A deliberate effort has to be made to relate the church to the local culture, to reorient its ways of thought and life, and if need be, to repattern the structure of the local church so as to identify it with the traditional heritage of the land. The emphasis on the "supra-national character of missions" should not neglect to reckon with the growing reality of national churches. The tendency of world confessional organizations is to generalize. It is difficult for them to realize that Asian and African countries do not all conform to a single pattern, nor do they accept a common pattern of political, social, and economic change for their nation building. What applies to one country does not apply to others. This is the day of the welfare state, and the service projects of the church are under severe trial. If they are to survive, they should prove their inherent worth as indispensable service agencies. They may not any longer be regarded, directly or indirectly, as instruments of evangelism. Decisions with regard to continuing them or discontinuing them, under these circumstances, will have to be reached by the entire Christian enterprise of any given Asian country with particular reference to the conditions that prevail in that country. The pressure of world confessional organizations, however, makes such united local decisions difficult.

Leaders of the younger churches who met together recently in Bangalore, India, in connection with the East Asia Christian Conference, drew pointed attention to this. It was their opinion that, "However good the intention, it seems that the expression of world confessionalism, in increasingly complex institutional structures, results in the perpetuation and reinforcement of patterns of paternalism and continued exercise of control." They went on further to add, "In a world confessional organization the younger churches will remain almost permanently weaker partners. The strength of the younger churches lies in increasing their missionary consciousness. A sense of this missionary responsibility goes hand in hand with an urgent sense of church unity. In the confessional perspective this remains out of focus. There is certainly strength in putting the resources of a whole confessional family behind its missionary concern, but the success of missionary work does not so much depend on the resources behind it as on its origin in the actual life of the Church where it is set. It is this present tension between the development of world confessionalism and the movement towards Church unity and Church co-operation which is a matter of serious concern." [1]

The three primary concerns of pressing urgency to Asian and African churches are unity, indigenization, and evangelism. Over against these are three new factors in the environment—nationalism, the resurgence of non-Christian religions, and social revolution. This has been said at the risk of oversimplification, but it has been stated with a view of bringing into relief the outstanding features of the situation. Any trend towards a revival, in the narrower sense of preserving traditional values, whether of denominationalism, of patterns of church life, or of narrow exclusivism in Christian beliefs and practice is a deterrent. Similarly, if there is any impression given of any sort of paternal pressure from outside, however disguised, in order to shape the think-

---

[1] *The World Confessional Development and the Younger Churches.* Statement by the East Asia Christian Conference, Bangalore, India, Nov. 12, 1961.

ing of the younger churches, it is resented as a relic of the passing order of colonialism. Also, if the claims of the Christian faith are not presented with direct relevance to the local situation in each one of these countries, particularly as bearing on the social ferment, evangelism in its comprehensive sense becomes obscurantist and meaningless. By giving world organizational expression to confessional loyalties, churches in Asia would seem to fall into the danger of becoming isolated, introspective, and pietistic.

CHAPTER 6

Christian Contributions to Nation Building

THE changing conditions of life in Southern Asia demand that we rethink our ideas about service. One thing is clear. The underlying motive in all Christian service is to point men to Christ. Serving mankind is integral to the Christian mission. It must not be separated from "proclaiming Christ in the ardent expectation that men will become His disciples and responsible members of His Church." At the same time Christians should not regard service as a means to an end. They should not give room to the misunderstanding that hospitals and schools are intended to induce people to become Christians.

From past experience in the field of Christian service have come some valuable lessons. For example, in many areas service agencies have been set up that involve wasteful duplication. In great part this has been due to denominational differences. It seems as if every denomination would like to run a school or a hospital in the same area. Some of this duplication has been obviated recently by the new trend toward co-operation. But more needs to be done in the direction of union institutions. Unfortunately, as already noted, supporting mission boards find that securing assistance from Christians in Europe, Great Britain, and especially America is difficult in the case of union institutions. A Methodist in the United States or a Congregationalist in Britain or a Lutheran in Sweden is more willing to give help to a school or a hospital maintained by his own particular denomination.

Beyond denominational co-operation in establishing service agencies, there is a need for over-all planning and co-ordination in terms of the total situation in any one area. What has been done so far is to develop strong denominational enterprises into co-operative union undertakings. More efforts have been made to pool resources than to discover whether projects fit into the total scheme of things. In over-all planning the determining factors should be to discover centers of greatest human need and to assess the combined ability of Christians to meet that need. The real question is, what forms of service are called for in terms of the greatest need? In answering this question, planners should bear in mind that the form of service as well as the greatest need of the place are best determined in close consultation with the people in that place. This has not often been the case in the past. Also, Christians need to be willing to admit that these forms of service and areas of need are subject to change from time to time.

Today India, Pakistan, and Ceylon have strong National Christian Councils. They are constantly giving thought to the best way Christian institutions can meet human needs. In such mutual consultation, representatives of both the younger and older churches are involved. The situation is different in each country, but everywhere the state is assuming more and more responsibility for the welfare of the people. Many long range plans with carefully formulated priorities have been developed. In a great number of these projects the co-operation of more industrialized countries of the world has been secured, with both monetary aid and technical assistance being advanced. For this reason, the whole idea of co-operation by Asian churches with their governments in service projects has changed radically. Moreover, it is now possible for Christians in the lands of the older churches not only to give monetary assistance themselves but to persuade their national governments to give such help. It is also possible for committed Christians in these lands to give service as "non-professional missionaries," or technical advisers.

In the past Asian Christians have not been involved in their society to any great degree. Many have viewed Christians who took an active part in politics as too worldly and perhaps as not very loyal Christians. But today men and women of the younger generation are convinced that they should not hesitate to take active part in the political life of their country if, as Christians, they want to serve their fellowmen.

POLITICAL PARTICIPATION

In India a series of conferences have been held by young leaders in the church in various parts of the country to arouse a sense of political responsibility among the Christians. The main findings of these conferences have been compiled by the young Indian Christian leader, M. M. Thomas. This significant book is aptly titled *Christian Participation in Nation Building*.[1] The major purpose of the conferences was to find out how Christians could best relate themselves to government plans for the development of their country. Young

[1] Available from World Council of Churches, Inc., 475 Riverside Drive, Rm. 439, N.Y. 27, N.Y., price $2.00.

Christian leaders in Ceylon also have been giving serious thought to contemporary affairs in their country.

The conviction is growing among many observers that the Christian minorities have a distinctive contribution to make to the development of the nations of Southern Asia through political participation. Of course, some Christians in these lands have spoken up when occasion arose, either in defense or in criticism of state policy. In Ceylon, for example, when the national language policy of the Sinhalese majority created an acute conflict with the Tamil minority, Ceylonese Christians intervened. In Kerala, when the Communist regime proposed state measures that threatened the freedom of the individual, Christians joined the liberation movement in large numbers and helped to throw the pro-Communist officials out of office and to elect more democratic representatives.

The church, as the church, should not identify itself with any political party or program, of course, but individual Christians should be free to take a stand. In Asian lands, however, it is not helpful to form a Christian political party. What is needed is for interested groups of Christians to undertake the responsibility of creating an informed public opinion. In India, for instance, Christians have been publishing a national weekly paper, the *Guardian*, for several decades. Its purpose is to keep Indian Christians informed on political events and to alert them to Christian action for the good of the nation.

The issues that Christians need to watch most closely are those concerning the rights of minorities, religious freedom, and undue governmental regulation of the lives of citizens. There is a Christian responsibility to safeguard and develop democratic political institutions. In the final analysis, any system of government is bound to stand or fall on three simple tests. One, does the system develop a sense of community among its people? Second, does it succeed in freeing the people from economic slavery and want? And third, does it preserve the basic liberties of individuals and groups within the nation? Many Asian Christians believe that a democratic form of government best meets these tests. Such views, indeed, were recorded at the East Asia Christian Conference held in Kuala Lumpur, Malaya, in 1959. Conferees agreed that:

The challenge before the East Asian countries is to find an indigenous and dynamic form of democracy. It is not necessary to adopt patterns worked out in the different circumstances of Western society; but our forms should provide a strong government committed to national integration and national development, and, at the same time, a government answerable to the people. Furthermore, for the success of any system of democracy and to achieve economic and social progress, men have to enter into meaningful relationships. For this purpose a web of voluntary associations is necessary. This will give rise to a pluralistic society in which people can overcome the vacuum and rootlessness that have resulted from the breaking up of old patterns and ideas. We may also stress at this stage the extreme importance of exploring and evaluating the cultural past of the great religions in this area, in order to set forth in greater relief the ethical values in them that have relevance to a national search for freedom and social justice. Indigenous cultural foundations are necessary for the emergence and sustenance of a healthy democratic secular society.

There is a problem, of course, in trying to build a sense of national coherence in a short span of time. Southern Asian society has existed for so long on traditional views of separate communities that to weld the peoples of each country into a single nation is most difficult, although of pressing concern. Another problem arises from the rapid transformation of an agricultural economy with a feudal social structure into an industrialized economy wherein feudalistic patterns are inappropriate. The introduction of small scale industries has gone a long way toward developing the economic life of the village, but there is a need for further land reform measures. In the transformation of the economy, aid from abroad has been helpful. There is increasing suspicion, however, that such assistance may involve political considerations. This has led to some amount of misunderstanding. There is always a danger, too, that economic aid and technical assistance may do serious damage to old patterns of life if they are not given with a real understanding of community needs. There is a Christian responsibility here: to make clear the nature of the concern of the more privileged nations of the West, on the one hand, and to interpret the reality of the needs of the underdeveloped lands of Asia, on the other. Meeting such a challenge calls for co-operation as between equals.

There are many areas of tension among the countries of Southern Asia. There is still the vexing issue between India and Pakistan over the political future of Kashmir. There is a question between Ceylon and India over the rights of Indian Tamils on the plantations of Ceylon. Pakistan and Afghanistan have been involved in border disputes, as have India and China, and a number of contrary pressures create problems for Nepal. This is to mention only a few instances. Nonetheless, there is at the same time a conscious feeling that Southern Asia, or all of Asia for that matter, should work together. In part this is a defense reaction; Asian solidarity is the one hope that could possibly prevent the revival of any Western colonial domination, in whatever form it might return. One of the reasons why Asians question military pacts and alliances with Western powers is just this fear of the possible return of colonialism. One of the contributions that world Christianity can make is to dispel this fear.

SOCIAL PERSPECTIVES

These lands of Southern Asia are described as areas of rapid social change. It is difficult to convey all that is meant by these words. It is not merely the evidences of technological advance and economic development that represent the revolutionary change. New standards of human values, with consequent disruption in social institutions, such as family and caste, have brought about considerable emotional upheaval also. Many parts of the traditional social structure are in the process of disintegration. It would not be true to say that Asian people have been swept off their feet by the new forces of industrialism, science and technology, and contemporary secularism. Resistance to change by reactionary and traditional forces has been no less pronounced. In this period of violent transition, new social structures, new patterns of human relations, and new standards of moral judgment are yet in the making.

In this context of change in South Asia, the need is twofold: The first is short-term, the other is long range. One aspect involves measures of social reform, the other social action. Social reform seeks to meet immediate need, and is of the nature of ambulance work. First aid in medicine brings relief to present suffering, it does not cure the disease. People dislocated by the impact of world forces on traditional life undoubtedly require palliatives by way of social reform. But there is a need to probe deeper into the causes of the social malady in order to treat the disease. In other words, the total social structure has to be repatterned in terms of human rights and social justice.

In the days of Mahatma Gāndhi temple doors were thrown open to the outcaste. When he got inside the sanctuary, however, he was made to feel so uncomfortable that he preferred not to go into the temple at all. Today the Indian Constitution makes all caste discrimination punishable by law. Temple entry offered relief, but to restore health to the society and establish the rights of the individual it was necessary to go further and remold the entire caste fabric. Similarly, social reform measures were initiated to help secure personal status for women in Hindu society, but it was left to the Parliament of Free India to put on its law books the Hindu Code Bill that today gives Hindu women the same rights in ownership, inheritance, and marriage contracts that had been so long the prerogative of Hindu men. Several such instances can also be cited for Pakistan and Ceylon, whose governments recognize the need for social action as well as social reform. The long range program aims at the reconstruction of society, while the short range program has social rehabilitation as its objective.

The Christian churches in Asian lands need to take

account of social action by governments in formulating their own plans for Christian service, especially since new forces of economic development, industrial progress, and modern social concepts are transforming the traditional social institutions that have been so long embedded in the feudal economy of predominantly rural cultures.

The economic development of South Asian lands depends on more agricultural production, even more industrial output, and upon increased trade with other Asian neighbors and the rest of the world. The new wealth acquired by such means could then be properly distributed. There are millions who are looking for regular wages and a reasonable livelihood. If they are to be provided for soon, there must be responsible economic planning. Each national government has to do this, and there is a reservoir of natural wealth and human resources to make this possible. What is required at the moment is technical assistance from abroad.

Asian governments have set up certain clear economic objectives already. One is the abolition of the old land holding patterns in agriculture. Pakistan, for example, has recently made remarkable progress in land reform. The generally accepted principle is one of private ownership by the farmers who work the land themselves. Absentee landlordism is severely condemned. Other governments provide rural financing, distribution of improved seeds and fertilizers, and technical advice to farmers. In spite of all these efforts, South Asian countries have not yet succeeded in becoming self-sufficient in food production, nor have they to any extent overcome rural unemployment.

Measures for increasing food production are very important because of rapid population growth. To meet this problem, land reform plans should come to grips with the traditional pattern of land holding. In India and Ceylon land has been divided according to family custom into small bits that make profitable farming by peasant owners impossible. Only co-operative farming can ensure the best utilization of fragmented land and scattered resources.

The development of co-operative farming can raise many questions. What about incentive and initiative, as well as the rights of private ownership? Christians have to give serious thought to these questions. Should the church encourage its members to take part in a program of rural co-operatives? Should they themselves set an example in land reform? These are very real questions in our countries. For instance, in India, the government is making real progress in land tenure schemes, rural credit facilities, marketing, and village development. But all these measures do not seem to solve the food problem. National leaders are therefore advocating co-operative farming. Side by side with these programs, the government is attempting to develop small scale industries in order to make village folk self-supporting and to provide employment for the surplus rural population.

By far the most important factor in the economic development of Southern Asia, however, is rapid industrialization. This is imperative, if the growing population, which cannot live by farming, is to find other means of livelihood. More and more attention is being given in economic planning to the development of heavy industry. Government leaders also are concerned with capital accumulation, facilities for the training of technicians and business executives, and a balanced industrial economy that deals adequately with the many new social problems arising from the development of an urban, industrial culture. All this is by no means easy. There are many hard choices: Should there be capital accumulation or expansion of welfare services? Should there be a priority on industrial goods or consumer goods? Then, again, there are acute situations created by the movement of vast numbers of people into the strange environment of the new industrial centers, involving the "inhuman break-up of village societies and the creation of disorderly aggregations of urban units."

Another area of concern is the rapid population increase in Asian countries. It not only puts a strain on food resources and marketing facilities but poses acute problems in areas of high population density. Leaders in various Asian countries are giving much attention to these questions. In India, Pakistan, and Ceylon, the governments are taking active interest in family planning and in promoting research to find new and suitable methods of birth control.

Christian churches are called to give positive guidance in this matter not only to their own members but also to other people. That some churches do not encourage even a discussion of these questions is itself a problem. At the Kuala Lumpur meeting of the East Asia Christian Conference, Asian Christian leaders stated:

We affirm that limitation of the size of the family is a decision to be reached responsibly by husband and wife. It is obligatory for educational agencies in this field to aim their programs at men as well as women. There can be good Christian reasons for limiting the family, apart from demographic considerations of controlling population. Considerations of family welfare must be regarded as supreme. To belittle the family in the interest of general population control is by Christian standards a sin.

Promotion of health programs go hand in hand with economic development. In Asia public health cannot be left entirely to voluntary agencies and individual action. It is the rightful concern of the state. But the Christian community should help supplement government programs wherever possible. Churches can also help to educate public opinion in regard to specific problems of public health such as leprosy and tuberculosis.

It must be freely admitted that economic development in Southern Asian countries is hindered by outworn cultural and social forces that are still active in community life. The lingering hold of caste and communal loyalties still restrict the freedom of the individual to change his occupation and to venture into new patterns of employment. The traditional attitudes toward life and toward work, to which religious orthodoxy lends support, inhibit the kind of positive action and progressive outlook that industrial society demands. In some places the process of change has led to confusion about moral standards, with resulting corruption in public and private life. Women still suffer social disabilities in many areas. Here the church can take a strong stand, for the improved status of women is a vital concern. Where religious factors underlie such restraints it is one of the urgent theological and sociological tasks of the church to interpret Christian teaching regarding the place of women in the home, the community, and the nation.

The establishment of innumerable factories has radically unsettled the total life of millions of former agricultural workers who have turned overnight into industrial laborers. The nature of work in these modern factories is entirely different from work on the farm or in cottage industries. Thanks to modern technology, factory work tends to become monotonous, fragmented, and apparently less creative. Moreover, the factory system does violence to community life. The relationship between employer and employee and even among employees themselves is depressingly impersonal. Overcome by loneliness and isolation, the new urban worker goes home to his village periodically, but is drawn back to the factory by the lure of higher wages—and all that money can buy.

Modern industrial work requires technical training that is very different from the kind of family apprenticeship that traditional crafts provided. It also calls for a new type of social discipline; for instance, the ability to work in co-ordination with hundreds of other workers on the assembly line. One has to be quick and alert, stick closely to a timetable, and work steadily until the end of the shift. This distinction between established working hours and leisure time is something totally new to village folk. Again, the place a laborer lives is different from the place where he works. It is not so in the village; there people work at home. Working in congested, ill-ventilated and unhygienic factories and living in crowded quarters that are often more like slums seriously affect the health and personal well-being of the workers. What is worse, for want of healthy recreational facilities, they fall prey to the temptations of commercial vice so common in the new urban culture.

The transition from rural to industrial patterns of life cuts both ways. It creates new opportunity for growth of independent selfhood, but at the same time it produces new forms of destructive pressure upon personality. The desperate loneliness of city life, the cramping bondage of organized industry, the meaninglessness of mechanical drudgery and lack of creativity in routine work, all these take heavy toll.

Technological change has also visibly influenced rural life. Industrial cities draw the younger and more adventurous men away from the villages, disrupting family and community life. The interdependence which held the village together is gone. It is no longer a self-contained unit of production and consumption. Now it imports goods and services from other places. Money-economy, road transport, and radio communication have made a world of difference. The family has also been affected in various ways. Men go to the industrial towns, leaving behind their wives and children. This frequently leads to disruption and disharmony in family life. Where the whole family migrates to a city, the women folk also find employment. The new independence and the added income create further problems within the family. Ethical decisions once made within the framework of an intimate village community are now left in modern industrial society to the individual. Now that customary sanctions are lifted, moral choice becomes ambiguous. In his new environment the industrial worker looks to the many new social groups that set the pattern for urban conduct, such as trade unions and other labor organizations.

Union organizations are popular for many reasons. The worker finds that trade unions help to protect his rights and prevent the employer from exploiting his ignorance. They make possible collective bargaining for fair wages and better working hours. More than all, they provide a sense of fellowship and community in the lostness and anonymity of modern industrial society. Labor organizations will inevitably play an increasingly important role in the economic and social development of the countries of Southern Asia. Christian leaders need to be more aware of the problems and the struggles of these movements. Only then can they understand and relate themselves to the creative thinking of the masses of the people in their countries. What is more, they should help produce adequate and able leadership from among the workmen themselves and lend active support to the programs of these organizations. Indifference to the problems of industrial workers and of farm laborers is still one of the fundamental weaknesses of the churches in Asia today, however.

"It is our conviction that the churches should be deeply involved in the whole process of economic and community development," writes M. M. Thomas. "Otherwise all talk of moral and spiritual values will remain unrelated to the technical and social realities of the situation. . . . The churches have pioneered in creating new forms of community life, and now that the nation is alive to the new possibilities they should make their contribution within the total national movement as it seeks to build community on a new basis. They cannot leave the field to the state and its experts."

CHAPTER 7

Christ's Mission and Ours

T HE present world situation is in many ways unprecedented. Rapid changes have overtaken every sphere of life. In consequence, the imperative demand everywhere is for a total change in patterns of thinking and modes of action. This applies particularly to the Christian missionary enterprise. Christians have come to the end of one epoch in world life. The new era into which they now enter is undoubtedly the product of God's activity in human history and in the world of nature. It is not merely the outcome of the natural course of events. Christian believers are called today to a three-fold venture of faith. In the first place, through careful re-study of the Scriptures, they should discover the nature and purpose of the Christian mission. Secondly, Christians need a clearer understanding of the relation of the Christian church to the gospel of the kingdom. Thirdly, there should be a concerted effort made to discover the ways in which God is at work in this very present hour for the redemption of the world.

Serious study and thinking on these three aspects of the Christian mission are already underway and lead directly back to the tremendous affirmation of biblical faith: "God so loved the world that he gave his only Son that whoever believes in him should not perish but have eternal life."

The Christian mission is founded on this revolutionary fact of Christ. Through his life, death, and resurrection, the redeeming power of God has been released into the stream of world history. In consequence, the entire creation is being redirected and transformed so that it may fulfill the purpose for which it was made. With the coming of Christ, the world and all in it are being made anew. The Incarnation is the beginning of a new creation. This new life is offered to every man. The new world is already present, here and now. The old order gives place to the new as world-life becomes increasingly

God-centered and, to that extent, less and less man-centered.

Essentially the good news to the world, made known in Jesus Christ, is that human self-centeredness, which is the root-sin of mankind and sets man in rebellion against the divine purpose for creation, has been destroyed. "The Kingdom of God is at hand." This is the work of God in Christ. The Risen Lord is the divine demonstration of this new life, now made possible to men of faith. It is a free gift, but a costly gift. It represents the humiliation and suffering of the Cross of Christ. To appropriate it for oneself is also costly. For the response of faith to the offer of the new life in Christ calls for willing obedience and total commitment. This is by no means easy. For it involves sharing in the suffering of our Lord in and for the world, now and until the end of time.

The insight of Christian thought and experience is that this new life is a true fellowship with God and with one another. It never exists in isolation as a peculiar gift to one individual apart from others. Just as the self-centeredness of man cannot be in any sense wholly individual, no more can the new life of a God-centered being be experienced and possessed by individuals alone.

The new life is in the world, not outside it. The declaration of the good news is not only an affirmation of the possibility of transformation but also an acknowledgment of the fact of change, as demonstrated in the life and work of those who have appropriated the gift of God in Christ. Therefore, the church is in fact the "first fruits" of the new creation. In this sense the church is an integral part of the gospel. It is the sign of triumphant grace that is made visible and actual in the life of each local Christian congregation in every nation. Within that fellowship, the Spirit is continually at work in order that the distinctive quality of Christian life, the new creation, may become more and more manifest. As long as these local communities of the faithful, scattered in different parts of the world, are bound by human ties to structures of life in creation, they also form part of the unredeemed world. So the work of transformation is still to be finally perfected.

Nevertheless, it is in this very context of the whole world, still in bondage to that self-centeredness that rebels against the eternal purpose of God being fulfilled in creation, which the Christian community is called to serve. Through such service, the church is being used as an instrument to communicate to the world of men the saving purpose of God in creation. The church is first and foremost a missionary community, participating in the missionary purpose of God himself, showing forth in its own life the first fruits, forecasting the harvest of the new age.

In every period of history the church is called to

reassess its tasks. In the first place it needs to become alive to the tremendous fact that God is at work in contemporary life, and, therefore, the final fulfillment of his purpose is assured. The entire creation is in fact being directed toward the achievement of the new order. To the discerning eye of faith, the passage of time in history is a "triumphant procession" toward the City of God. To those who have eyes to see the coming kingdom, it is a constant reminder of the abiding faithfulness of these promises of God in Christ.

In the revolutionary changes of our time, there is undoubtedly the feverish activity of man seeking to realize ends of his own making and defying the will of God for his creation. But in and through that very revolutionary context of life, God also is redemptively at work for the fulfillment of his purpose. Christian faith may not be able to distinguish clearly between what is of God and what is of man in any dynamic situation. It only rests assured that in every situation in contemporary life, despite human perversity, God's will must eventually prevail. It is this affirmation we repeat at the end of the prayer that our Lord taught his disciples: "For thine is the kingdom and the power and the glory, forever."

The Christian's awareness of God's persisting concern in human history is due to the creative work of the Holy Spirit in his own life. He has in himself experienced the amazing wonder of God's forgiveness set forth for all mankind on Calvary. Whereas, before he was blind, he now sees. ". . . for mine eyes have seen thy salvation which thou hast prepared in the presence of all peoples, a light for revelation to the Gentiles, and for glory to thy people Israel" (Luke 2:30-22).

Therefore, since the day of Pentecost, the compulsion to testify to the gospel of the kingdom has gathered force with spontaneous urgency in the lives of those who have been shaken by the power of the Risen Lord. God himself creates this response of faith in men's hearts through the Holy Spirit. The apostolic mandate is to every man that he be a disciple, ". . . you shall be my witnesses. . . ." (Acts 1:8). "As the Father has sent me, even so I send you" (John 20:21). Our task in missionary witness is to proclaim this message of hope in our Lord: that in Jesus Christ, God is reconciling the world to himself. In Jesus Christ, peace is made between God and man; between man and his neighbor; and between man and his own self.

THE CONTENT OF THE WITNESS

Both biblical authority and Christian experience are agreed on four fundamental assertions of Christian faith that furnish the claim and content of the good news to which we witness:

First, the whole creation, life in totality, every aspect

of earthly existence, will be brought eventually under the direct sway of God "according to his purpose which he set forth in Christ as a plan for the fullness of time, to unite all things in him, things in heaven and things on the earth" (Eph. 1:9-10).

Second, the message of the kingdom, in a special sense, is directed to the individual and collective conscience of mankind. If God's purpose for his creation is delayed, it is because man, as no other creature, rebels against God's will being done. Man's sinfulness is the chief deterrent. By accepting the assurances of God's forgiveness, offered in Jesus Christ, men become converted from rebellion to obedience through repentance and faith.

Third, this work of redemption is in fact being carried out—now and everywhere in our world. It is a present occurrence.

Fourth, in the fulfillment of his purpose, God is making use of men who respond in faith to the imperious "Follow me" of the Master who assures them, "Fear not, for I will make you fishers of men."

When men are convinced of God's redemptive purpose in their lives, they discover their true vocation. They find their calling as "witnesses," working together with God and with other men in the fellowship of the church to fulfill God's purpose for his creation. Witnessing to the faith is in a sense peculiarly characteristic of Christian belief. No one can claim to be a Christian believer unless he bears living testimony to the redemptive work of God in Christ Jesus as a present reality. Thus evangelistic witness, which is at the same time, and for all times, a cosmic process, a divine activity, a historic reality, and a people's movement, is missionary in origin and intention, and congregational in purpose and design. It is both a going forth and a gathering in.

WHERE THE MISSION IS

In considering the missionary task of the church in the world today, it is apparent that it is no longer possible to group the various countries of the world into two watertight compartments labeled Christian and non-Christian. Today there are many people of other faiths and of no faith in Christian lands, as in other parts of the world. Every church finds itself in a missionary situation. It is set in a non-Christian context, even in so-called Christian countries. Thus the base of missionary action is the total church itself. Secondly, with the growth and establishment of the church in Asia and Africa, there has come about a change in the relationship between the younger churches and the older churches. Now we are all partners together in a common task.

In every land the church is a missionary community. It has specific responsibilities in its national setting and in the peculiar circumstances of its placement. There is a task now for each church—for the churches in India and Pakistan just as much as for the churches in the United States and Canada, for example. But on the other hand, churches everywhere are called together in a total missionary effort to the whole world. This is the basis for the call to ecumenical mission, and it can only be met in planning and working together. This means, above all, that the church in each country should discover for itself how best it can fulfill its task—just where it is placed in the world. It should be in creative relationship with the life and the culture of the people around it. Man's social existence ties him together with others in relationships that are political and cultural. If the local community of Christians in any nation does not form a real part of the environment in which it is placed, it makes no impact on the people around it. The temptation so far has been for Christians to live in isolation, as a people apart. This has been referred to as the "ghetto mentality" of the Christian minority.

The need for the church to become indigenous is made all the more imperative by modern social forces. If the church is not quick to respond to these changes, and is itself uninvolved in them, it ceases to possess the ability to communicate the gospel. It leaves no impact upon the changing intellectual and cultural currents of modern life. More than all, the church becomes mean-

ingless and irrelevant, especially to the rising generation of men and women who hold the future in their
hands.

But how much energy is consumed in drives and cam-
paigns to consolidate the traditional patterns of institutional life! More often than not, local communities
of Christians, instead of being outreaching and mission-
ary-minded, have become self-centered and self-contained. Conformity to the world may spell success, as
the world measures success, in terms of numerical expansion, material possessions, and social prestige. Conformity
to the Lord of the churches would mean going the way
he himself went, the way of humiliation, suffering, and
apparent defeat. That way leads to the new life in the
kingdom. Moreover, the church can penetrate the
indifference of its secular environment to fulfill its
mission only when it sets forth in its local expression the
visible marks of genuine and dynamic community. The
congregation that God uses to communicate the gospel
is a community constrained by the love of Christ to
share this experience with others. In the lands of the
younger churches, we are constantly reminded that the
outsider becomes inquisitive and asks questions concerning the faith only when the impact of Christian communion is felt on the group life of the traditionally
ordered society.

The fact that the ministry of Christian witness is exercised in the world calls for identification with the present concerns of secular life. Christians are called to live *with* their fellowmen, and yet as different *from* them. It is here that the crucial role of the Christian layman in the missionary witness of the church needs to be re-emphasized. There is still too much of the professional in the church's ministry that alienates the common folk of farm, factory, and market place. There is such a thing as "gossiping the gospel," the spontaneous ease that communicates the gospel in terms of everyday concerns. This is by no means a new discovery. It is the way that simple Christian people spread the good news of the kingdom in the early centuries of Christian history. If the gospel is to become intelligible and relevant to the common man in the modern world, it, too, must be through a church that is truly indigenous. It can grow in Southern Asia and elsewhere only through witnesses who think and speak and behave like those with whom they communicate.

This means that, together with their Lord, the people of God must go forth to modern man where he is in his world of work, in his family life, and in his leisure activities. There in the work-a-day world, Christians must learn to meet and talk with modern man—talking together as contemporary men—with the pressures of secularism upon them, with poverty for many a paramount and endless worry, with problems of choice to face daily, with a crying need to find some meaning in existence.

Out of the wealth of experience, living with the village folk of India, a missionary *sadhu*, holy man, has stated, "It is more than possible that the word, God, or the name Jesus Christ, or theological ideas will not be mentioned; but whatever our common endeavor, the Living God will be there, and the word of Divine Grace will be there. The validity of the Christian faith will not be in my hands but in the hands of God, the Holy Spirit, who will be between us as we meet."

THE LAY WITNESS

One of the far-reaching changes in the understanding of the church is the recognition of the place of the layman. Traditionally every congregation came to think of itself as organized around the minister. The laity, the people of God, were subordinated to the minister, helping in various ways, but not responsible participants in the life and work of the church. In our day we have learned that the local congregation is an interdependent group of dedicated people, to *each* of whom God has given gifts of grace. It is important that the structure of congregational life should permit the best use of the special gifts of each member to build the household of God and fulfill the missionary calling of the church. This can lead to a revolutionary renewal of congregational life.

The need for a more active laity has drawn attention to the necessity for a smaller unit of fellowship such as the "house-church." Effective forces of Christian influence can radiate into the community and into the world from such small groups. But these smaller units of Christian men and women must be nurtured in the faith so that in daily contact with other people their lives and work may effectively communicate the faith whereby they live. At the same time, drawn together by frequent acts of corporate worship and the observance of the sacrament of the Lord's Supper, they can maintain their relationship with the larger fellowship of the parish. There would, of course, still be need for a special full time ministry by men who have special gifts for building up the whole congregation. Their main task would be not organization and administration but "transforming the congregation into a dynamic spiritual community in which each member recognizes and uses his particular gift for service in the church and in the world."

In addition to evangelizing the neighborhood, the local church has also the responsibility of crossing cultural and national boundaries to carry the message of hope to "the ends of the world." There is still, and there always will be, those to whom a specific call has been given to venture out beyond their neighborhood across the seas to people far away. Such a missionary call, when it comes to them, every local congregation must help to fulfill, for through their vision the church reaches out, and with them it goes forth to the world. But today we know that such missionary vocation is not given solely to those so long described as "professional missionaries." Doctors and teachers, men and women giving technical assistance in village and city, as well as students in quest of knowledge and wider experience, are constantly crossing cultural and national borders. They, too, have the task of Christian witness wherever they are placed, exercising on new frontiers and in new ways the missionary calling of the Christian fellowship. In and through them God in Christ is exercising his ministry of reconciliation and redemption.

THE CHURCHES TOGETHER

While each church in each country has its peculiar task of witness, there is also a special task for all churches to do together. Christians now recognize, as never before in modern times, the essential oneness of the members of the body of Christ, as well as the fundamental missionary character of the church. This awareness is the outcome of the ecumenical movement of our times, and it is changing all thinking and planning about the mission of the church in and to the world. One thing is clear: it is impossible to carry out the Christian mission except in unity as one body.

Another change in mission strategy is the realization

that the base of missionary operation is no longer in the so-called Christian lands of Europe and North America. Missions to other countries, planned, directed, and manned from Britain and the United States, for instance, are now outdated and ineffective. Another thing to be borne in mind is the supreme need of man in modern technological culture to build a world community. People of the world ask whether the Christian mission is helping to foster and sustain this growing sense of the solidarity of mankind. In saying this we must not forget that at all costs the biblical emphasis that Jesus Christ is the Lord of history and the one hope of mankind should not be obscured in the preaching of the gospel and in service to others.

Unity in mission comes out of unity in purpose. And purpose relates to the end result, the final outcome, and not to immediate objectives. Christians are all agreed that evangelism is to make widely known what God in Christ has done, is doing, and will do for the world of men. But to what end is it all leading? That is the question for which the church needs to have a common answer. The divine purpose in Christ's mission is the ultimate consummation of his will for his creation. Christians say that it is "given," that the end is perfectly clear in God's own mind. He knows what he is about. Humans can only see the end result in part. They cannot, therefore, insist on general agreement about present methods and immediate objectives except that the final establishment of God's reign is an assured reality. God is even now at work, and his purpose will be realized not because of us, but in spite of us.

But the fact remains that Christians tend to be divided among themselves when they begin to formulate immediate goals. Division results out of preoccupation with one or another as if they were all mutually exclusive. In broad outline these immediate goals of evangelism seem to fall into three main groups: the reordering of world life through social action; the expansion of the fellowship of the church; and the proclamation of the truth as revealed in Christ Jesus in terms of a particular understanding of it.

Some evangelists hold that the immediate end is to help further the rapid social changes in which we all are involved. They interpret today's social evils as demonic forces, "principalities and powers," against which God is battling, and in that battle the Christian should take sides with God. Some of this group hold that in this enterprise co-operation is possible both among Christians themselves and with all other non-Christian agencies that work toward this same end. In all such common endeavor for social action, Christian men and women, representing churches ranging all the way from Roman Catholic formalism to Quaker simplicity, are working together in apparent accord. The basis of unity here is the least common denominator of the Christian creed. This is a temporary concession, however, for the confessional faith in each case is held in reserve, so the division actually persists underground. Moreover, for lack of serious thinking concerning the theology of the Christian mission, the basic distinction between the gospel and other faiths is blurred.

A church-centric program, on the other hand, aims primarily at the extension of the church. The intention is to bring into the church all men of other faiths and of no faith. Mass evangelism, both in post-Christian and in non-Christian cultures, concentrates on the numerical and geographical expansion of the church and frequently reverts to denominationalism. Propaganda and proselytism become mixed up with preaching and conversion; sometimes they break out in unseemly missionary rivalry. More frequently there is a needless duplication of work and consequent waste in resources.

Sectarianism is an exaggerated form of the church-centric type of missions. Here the immediate objective is to have men accept a particular creedal position that emphasizes certain specific doctrines as fundamental. Sectarianism seems to be erupting all over Southern Asia. It is a contemporary phenomenon that we Asians find impossible to check, since these enterprises are largely manned and directed by missionary agencies from abroad, especially the United States. Sometimes this sectarian type of evangelism is the work of free lance missionaries supported by those Christian groups whose primary intention seems to be to oppose communism. In any case, unity in mission is lost.

One of the best formulas for missionary co-operation was spelled out at the Faith and Order Conference held in Lund, Sweden, in 1952. "We should do together all things which our Christian conscience does not compel us to do separately." This means that Christians should courageously face all obstacles to unity. An encouraging development in this respect was the calling of the Second Vatican Ecumenical Council by the Church of Rome. On the other hand, co-operation with independent and sectarian groups is by no means easy. What is called for is a more charitable understanding and a more determined effort to draw into the larger unity of the church these splinter groups that are also greatly concerned in the same task of Christian witness. The missionary approach to the non-Christian world demands, as never before, that the church demonstrate in its own life the unity of Christ to which it invites others.

In terms of the new understanding of mission, the direction of missionary activity is shared in a real sense by both the younger and the older churches. But the significance of this partnership is still to be fully realized. The day-to-day members of local congregations in different churches all over the world do not yet share this conviction. To help them toward a wider perspective is the primary purpose of missionary education.

The relationship between the younger and the older churches is no longer the sole concern of missionary boards. Christian people everywhere should be encouraged to understand the meaning of their interdependence as the people of God on earth. For several generations Western Christians were brought up to believe that the Christian people in countries where the church had been newly established were in some sense dependent upon them. Missionaries had to be sent to these countries and had to be maintained there with special funds. Schools, hospitals, and churches established in foreign lands by these missionaries depended on Western support. Plans for expansion of work, the distribution of grants, and the general direction of policy in any given country were all made at what was called the "home base" through representatives of the mission's board. That was the age of paternalism in Christian missions.

As the churches in mission lands became more self-reliant, the tendency was to think in terms of independence. Various measures were adopted to promote such independence. The goal was to have the churches stand on their own feet, as it were, and was described as self-support. This meant not only that the churches in mission lands were to be able to meet their own bills but also to manage their own affairs. Undoubtedly the intention was good. To encourage dependence was to handicap growth. But the transition from dependence to independence frequently led to the unfortunate conclusion that the relationship had been cut off. Any further mutual interest would be of the nature of interference. This development resulted in increasing estrangement and indifference that cut at the roots of real fellowship among Christian people of the world. Neither dependence nor independence can further the mission of the whole church to the whole world. The future depends upon discovering the nature and substance of the interdependence of the younger and older churches in terms of the far-flung implications for the life and mission of the church.

In India, Pakistan, and Ceylon there are indigenous churches that are in varying measure autonomous. They own their church buildings, their ministers are children of the soil, their current expenses are mostly met from local resources, and they administer their affairs themselves. At the same time, in all these countries, relationships with missions from churches in Europe, Britain, and North America are maintained through continued assistance in men and money. Missionaries, both men and women, work as evangelists, parish ministers, teachers in schools and colleges, doctors and nurses in hospitals, and in various other ways. Substantial grants for carrying on the work of the church are also accepted and used both for capital and current expenses. Mission boards have a responsibility for their workers whose support and welfare are in a special sense their concern. They also owe it to the people from whom they receive their mission funds to see that they are wisely spent. Thus it happens that in each of these countries there are still mission ties to the churches that are supposedly more or less independent.

THE MISSION AND THE CHURCH

The goal now is to integrate mission and church so that they together form a whole. This involves a two-fold program. On the one hand, it means that the "mission" part of the older church—its missionary workers, its organizational machinery, and its financial administration—should become an integral part of the younger church. On the other hand, ways and means should be found to enable the older and the younger churches to press forward together in fulfilling their common missionary task. In such partnership each should learn to give and to receive according to ability and need. This is where interdependence becomes concretely manifest.

Now it is clear that this ideal presupposes a reasonably strong local church. It should be capable of initiative and possess sufficient maturity in the faith. It should be able to command adequate leadership and be in a position to make independent decisions when need arises. It should have an appreciable number of informed and active members. By and large all this may be true of the churches in India, Pakistan, and Ceylon if they are considered as a whole. But the fact remains that the whole consists of unevenly developed parts. There are areas in each of these lands where the church is highly developed, especially in urban centers. There are other areas, mostly rural, where the local church is still in its infancy. So while the process of integration goes on with imagination and understanding, steps must also be taken to strengthen the church where it is weak.

There are three main concerns in the integration of mission and church to which all of us of both the younger and older churches should give thought. The first is in the matter of mutual counseling and joint planning. The second relates to the sending and receiving of fellow workers. And the third is with regard to the use of funds provided for the mission work of the church. This last point has produced much heart-searching, and rightly so. It also has been the source of much misunderstanding. Total financial dependence does not mean interdependence. In confronting this problem of the proper use of funds, the East Asia Christian Conference has consistently followed a single principle. Unless an autonomous local church is willing itself to raise a fourth of the amount it asks for from other churches, it is discouraged from undertaking the project for which it seeks help. Moreover, it is generally accepted that financial aid from other churches should be sought primarily for projects that would strengthen the local church for its mission to the world.

A recent development in the churches in India and Ceylon has been the interest shown in sending missionaries from these countries to Indonesia, Thailand, Nepal, and to various countries in Africa. Such projects have been made possible by aid from other churches, both on a denominational basis and across denominational lines. This principle of giving help to strengthen the church so that it can carry on its mission to the world has to be applied with considerable foresight. The training of the ministry and the promotion of both literacy and literature are essentials. In this connection a tremendous amount of good can come from the generous grants made to theological institutions in India by the Theological Education Fund of the World Council of Churches. The real fruits of this program in terms of trained leadership and the production of theological literature will only be fully realized, however, two or three generations hence.

In every case there should be mutual counseling in this much desired growing together of church and mission. Joint discussion and study of needs and opportunities have proved immensely useful. Experience has shown that national councils of churches have contributed greatly to this new understanding. There are many able church leaders in Southern Asia and their considered opinions have guided the representatives of mission boards in each country as they co-operated in formulating policies and deciding on priorities with the needs and opportunities of the whole nation in view. All requests of mission board aid for co-operative projects now pass through the national Christian councils.

Denominational projects, of course, do not pass through the national councils since the relationship is unilateral. There is danger here that the exclusive provision of funds to a particular church within a given area may produce a number of problems, including the fostering of disunity and the smothering of ecumenical growth. This is the reason why the East Asia Christian Conference advises its member churches that when they want to make a survey of Christian service in any country they should view the situation as a whole. Only then can Asian Christians measure the part that the churches together play and make responsible judgments as to whether the best possible use is being made of the personnel and funds at their disposal, or whether strategy should be changed in view of the changing situation.

The churches in Southern Asia have been greatly helped by generations of able missionary men and women who have come from all parts of Europe, Great Britain, and North America. The foundations of the churches were laid by missionary fathers whose names are still held in affectionate memory in various parts of India, Pakistan, and Ceylon. It was inevitable that in the formation of these local churches missionary influence on the life and thought of the people would be dominant. The early converts looked up to the missionaries and were guided by their decisions in all matters. But over a century of missionary endeavor has passed into history and in the development of local churches, things have changed.

Perhaps the most powerful single factor of change is the passing of colonialism and the emergence of nation-states. The church confronts a new situation and needs a new kind of relationship to it. The traditional pattern of the missionary who came from the ruling races of the Christian West has given place to that of a fellow-worker who represents the anxious concern of another church to share with the local church their common responsibility to preach the gospel. Many young men and women in churches everywhere are called to this missionary vocation. They have the special gift of grace to cross national and cultural boundaries and go from their own church to another and there join forces for missionary witness. These dedicated youth come from churches the world around. They know the price they have to pay for their witness—giving up loyalties to family, culture, and nation in order to identify themselves with Christ's mission in this world. They know that when they go forth from their own church to another they are to be fully identified with the church of their adoption. And such identification involves tremendous effort that only the gift of God's Holy Spirit can make possible.

A grave responsibility rests on all of us who are members of the body of Christ to find the means that will enable these dedicated youth to fulfill their missionary calling. They go because we cannot go. They do what we cannot do. They are living links that forge together a world-wide Christian fellowship. They symbolize the vital concern we have in one another as different churches and in the missionary task of the whole church for the whole world. In this light missionary giving should be viewed as both a privilege and an obligation.

It is true that the patterns of service and the relationship of the workers who go out from one church to another may still have to change from time to time. Courageous experiments are in fact being made in both these matters. Serious thought is being given as to how best missionary fellow-workers can be taken into the life of the inviting local churches and given scope for fulfilling their missionary vocation. As long as the church lasts on earth, there will always be need for committed men and women who have a specific missionary vocation to go and help, crossing all barriers of culture, nationality, and race.

CHRISTIAN LAYMEN OVERSEAS

Side by side, in an increasingly interdependent secular world, there are opening up new possibilities for Christian service by "non-professional missionaries." An increasing number of Christian laymen are going from one country to another in various capacities in business and industry, technical assistance, and diplomatic service. "They do amazing things," one church report states, "in charity, social work, or church committees, in running groups, visiting, evangelising. A good deal more is done by the wives. With the great number of servants they can now have, they have more time for social service than at home. However, professing Christians are nevertheless few in number, too few for the vast task."

The fact is that most of the people who go out from Christian lands in the West do not have any missionary concern because they themselves are not believers. But this very fact also places a heavy responsibility on the small minority who are committed Christians and members of the church in their home lands. In India, for instance, Christian laymen should actively share in the task of Christian witness. The Christian from abroad manifests the universal character of our faith, a fact particularly important in the new situations in which Indians find themselves. Also, Christians from the West have had a wider and longer experience in an industrial society and can offer insight on the Christian response to technology. And finally, someone from outside, holding a responsible position, often has opportunities that are not open in the same way to Indian Christians.

Here is a potential for the life and mission of the church that should be taken seriously. For the fact remains that these same people, if they do not happen to be Christian, can do great damage to the missionary cause. On the other hand, if they come out with strong Christian convictions, they can be a tremendous asset for Christian witness and service. But it is necessary that they should be provided with opportunities for special preparation for this vocation, and that is the responsibility of their home church. The church in the land to which they go has also the responsibility of recognizing their presence in their midst and receiving them into the fellowship of the local Christian community, as well as providing them with opportunity for Christian witness.

Reading List

LEADERS of study groups may order the Friendship Press books listed below from denominational literature headquarters. From these same sources they may order the *Adult Guide on Southern Asia* by Maryruth Nickels, priced at 75 cents, which contains program plans for using *Christian Issues in Southern Asia* as well as other Friendship Press materials.

Books of other publishers are listed as additional resources. They are available in bookstores and libraries.

FRIENDSHIP PRESS BOOKS

Eastman, Addison J. *Branches of the Banyan: Observations on the Church in Southern Asia.* Eastern and Western writers comment on the variety and nature of Christian fellowship. Photos. 1963. Paper, $1.95.

Leard, G. Earl. *This Is Southern Asia*. An illustrated primer for youth and adults covering India, Pakistan, Ceylon, and Nepal. 1963. Paper, 85 cents.

Living Religions Series. *Introducing Buddhism* by Kenneth Scott Latourette, *Introducing Hinduism* by Malcolm Pitt, and *Introducing Islam* by J. Christy Wilson. Basic resources for Southern Asia. 1956–58. Paper, 90 cents.

Spencer, Steven and Mary. *Outposts of Medicine*. An experienced husband and wife writing team reports on medical missions. Includes a chapter on India and Pakistan. 1963. Paper, $1.25.

Stowe, David M. *When Faith Meets Faith*. A popularly written description of the world's major religions and possible Christian attitudes toward them. 1963. Paper, $1.95.

Taylor, Richard W. and Thomas, M. M. *Mud Walls and Steel Mills*. Interprets revolutionary India in the context of Christian theology. For students. 1963. Paper, $1.75.

Devanesen, Chandran. *The Cross Is Lifted*. Poems about India and her people. 1954. Paper, $1.25.

BOOKS OF OTHER PUBLISHERS

SOUTH ASIA—THE INDIAN SUBCONTINENT

Basham, Arthur Llewellyn. *The Wonder that Was India: A Survey of the Culture of the Indian Sub-Continent Before the Coming of the Muslims*. (Evergreen Encyclopedia, V. 1.) N.Y.: Grove Press, 1959. (Paper)

Birdwell, Lord. *Two Nations and Kashmir*. London: Robert Hale, Ltd., 1956.

Brown, Donald Mackenzie. *The White Umbrella; Indian Political Thought from Manu to Gandhi.* Berkeley: University of California, 1953. (Paper)

Brown, William Norman, ed. *India, Pakistan, Ceylon.* Ithaca, N.Y.: Cornell University Press, 1951.

——. *The United States and India and Pakistan.* Cambridge, Mass.: Harvard University Press, 1953.

De Bary, William Theodore and Others, comps. *Sources of the Indian Tradition.* N.Y.: Columbia University Press, 1958.

Edwardes, Michael. *A History of India from the Earliest Times to the Present Day.* N.Y.: Farrar, Straus & Cudahy, Inc., 1961.

Isaacs, Harold Robert. *Scratches on Our Minds: American Images of China and India.* N.Y.: John Day Co., Inc., 1958.

Karim, A. K. Nazmul. *Changing Society in India and Pakistan. . . .* N.Y.: Oxford University Press, 1956. (Paper)

Korbel, Josef. *Danger in Kashmir.* Princeton, N.J.: Princeton University Press, 1954.

Nawrath, Alfred. *Eternal India: The Land, the People, the Masterpieces of Architecture and Sculpture of India, Pakistan, Burma, and Ceylon.* N.Y.: Crown Publishers, 1956.

Nehru, Jawaharlal. *Discovery of India.* (Anchor Book.) N.Y.: Doubleday & Co., Inc., 1960. (Paper)

Panikkar, Kavalam Madhava. *A Survey of Indian History.* London: Meridian Books, Ltd., 1947.

Rawlinson, Hugh George. *A Concise History of the Indian People.* N.Y.: Oxford University Press, 1950. (Paper)

Riencourt, Amaury de. *The Soul of India.* N.Y.: Harper & Brothers, 1960.

READING LIST

Rowland, Benjamin. *The Art and Architecture of India*: *Buddhist, Hindu, Jain*. Baltimore: Penguin Books, Inc., 1953. (Paper)

Schmid, Peter. *India: Mirage and Reality*. N.Y.: Pitman Publishing Corp., 1961.

Sen, Gertrude (Emerson). *The Pageant of India's History*. N.Y.: Harper & Brothers, 1959. (Paper)

Shepherd, Gordon. *Where the Lion Trod*. N.Y.: The St. Martin's Press, Inc., 1961.

Spear, Percival. *India: A Modern History*. Ann Arbor, Mich.: University of Michigan Press, 1961.

Thomson, Ian. *Changing Patterns in South Asia*. N.Y.: Roy Publishers, 1962.

Wallbank, Thomas Walter. *A Short History of India and Pakistan* . . . . (Mentor.) N.Y.: The New American Library of World Literature, Inc., 1958. (Paper)

INDIA

Anand, Mulk Raj. *India in Colour . . . Photographs by Suzanne Hausammann*. N.Y.: McGraw-Hill Book Co., Inc., 1959.

Biardeau, Madeleine. *India*. (Vista Bks.) N.Y.: The Viking Press, Inc., 1960. (Paper)

Bowles, Chester. *Ambassador's Report*. N.Y.: Harper & Brothers, 1954.

Chakravarti, Prithwis Chandra. *India's China Policy*. Bloomington, Ind.: Indiana University Press, 1962.

Cormack, Margaret Lawson. *She Who Rides a Peacock: Indian Students and Social Change*. N.Y.: Frederick A. Praeger, Inc., 1962.

Dean, Vera Micheles. *New Patterns of Democracy in India*. Cambridge, Mass.: Harvard University Press, 1959.

READING LIST

Dube, Shyama Charan. *India's Changing Villages: Human Factors in Community Development.* Ithaca, N.Y.: Cornell University Press, 1958.

Filliozot, Jean. *India: The Country and Its Traditions.* Englewood, N.J.: Prentice-Hall, Inc., 1962.

Harrison, Selig S., ed. *India and the United States.* N.Y.: The Macmillan Co., 1961.

———. *India: The Most Dangerous Decades.* Princeton, N.J.: Princeton University Press, 1960.

India (republic). Planning Commission. *The New India: Progress Through Democracy.* N.Y.: The Macmillan Co., 1958. (Paper)

Lyon, Jean. *Just Half a World Away: My Search for the New India.* N.Y.: Thomas Y. Crowell Company, 1955.

Mehta, Ved Parkash. *Walking the Indian Streets.* Boston: Little, Brown & Co., 1960.

Moraes, Francis Robert (Frank). *India Today.* N.Y.: The Macmillan Co., 1960.

Nair, Kusum. *Blossoms in the Dust: The Human Factor in Indian Development.* N.Y.: Frederick A. Praeger, Inc., 1962.

Nehru, Jawaharlal. *Toward Freedom.* Boston: Beacon Press, Inc., 1958. (Paper)

Panikkar, Kavalam Madhava. *Common Sense About India.* N.Y.: The Macmillan Co., 1960.

Schmid, P. *India: Mirage and Reality.* Toronto: Clarke Irwin & Co., Ltd., 1961.

Seligman, Eustace. *What the United States Can Do About India.* N.Y.: New York University Press, 1956.

Smith, Bradford. *Portrait of India.* Philadelphia: J. B. Lippincott Company, 1962.

READING LIST

Trumbull, Robert. *As I See India*. N.Y.: William Sloane Associates, Inc., 1956.

Ward, Barbara. *India and the West*. N.Y.: W. W. Norton & Company, Inc., 1961.

Zinkin, Taya. *Caste Today*. N.Y.: Oxford University Press, 1962.

PAKISTAN

Asad, Muhammad. *The Principles of State and Government in Islam*. Berkeley: University of California Press, 1961.

Binder, Leonard. *Religion and Politics in Pakistan*. Berkeley: University of California Press, 1961.

Crescent and Green: A Miscellany of Writings on Pakistan. N.Y.: Philosophical Library, Inc., 1955.

Ferguson, James P. *Kashmir: An Historical Introduction*. London: Centaur Press, Ltd., 1962.

Ikram, S. M. and Spear, Percival, eds. *The Cultural Heritage of Pakistan*. N.Y.: Oxford University Press, 1955.

Khan, Liaquat Ali. *Pakistan: Heart of Asia*. Cambridge, Mass.: Harvard University Press, 1951.

Qureshi, Ishtiaq Husain. *The Pakistani Way of Life*. N.Y.: Frederick A. Praeger, Inc., 1956.

Toynbee, Arnold Joseph. *Between Oxus and Jumna*. N.Y.: Oxford University Press, 1961.

CEYLON

Bailey, Sidney D. *Ceylon*. London: Hutchinson & Co., Ltd., 1952. (Paper)

Blazé, Ray. *Ceylon: Its People and Its Homes*. Hollywood-by-the-Sea, Fla.: Transatlantic Arts, Inc., 1961.

READING LIST

Cuylenburg, Reg van. *Image of an Island; A Portrait of Ceylon.*
N.Y.: Orion Press, Inc., 1962.

Ludowyk, Evelyn F. C. *The Story of Ceylon.* London: Faber
and Faber, Ltd., 1962.

Tresidder, Argus J. *Ceylon: An Introduction to the Resplendent
Land.* Princeton, N.J.: Princeton University Press, 1960.
(Paper)

Williams, Harry William. *Ceylon: Pearl of the East.* N.Y.: The
Macmillan Co., 1956.

Wriggens, William Howard. *Ceylon: Dilemmas of a New Nation.*
Princeton, N.J.: Princeton University Press, 1960.

NEPAL

Bourdillon, Jennifer. *Visit to the Sherpas.* Toronto: William
Collins Sons & Co., Canada, Ltd., 1956.

Douglas, William O. *Beyond the High Himalayas.* N.Y.: Doubleday & Company, Inc., 1952.

Eskelund, Karl. *The Forgotten Valley: A Journey into Nepal.*
N.Y.: Taplinger Publishing Company, Inc., 1961.

Forbes, Duncan. *The Heart of Nepal.* Toronto: Thomas Allen,
Ltd., 1962.

Hagen, Toni, and Others. *Nepal.* Chicago: Rand McNally &
Company, 1961.

Hardie, Norman. *In Highest Nepal: Our Life Among the Sherpas.*
London: George Allen & Unwin, Ltd., 1955.

Leuchtag, Ericka. *Erika and the King.* N.Y.: Coward-McCann,
Inc., 1958.

Snellgrove, David Llewellyn. *Himalayan Pilgrimage . . . Through
Western Nepal.* London: Bruno Cassirer, Publishers, Ltd.,
1961.

READING LIST

Tilman, Harold William. *Nepal Himalaya.* London: Cambridge University Press, 1952.

Tucci, Giuseppe. *Nepal: The Discovery of the Malla.* N.Y.: E. P. Dutton & Co., Inc., 1962.

Weir, Thomas. *East of Katmandu.* (Essential Books.) N.Y.: Oxford University Press, 1956. (Paper)

FAITHS AND PHILOSOPHIES

Bayne, Stephen F., Jr. *Ceylon, North India, Pakistan: A Study in Ecumenical Decision.* London: Society for Promoting Christian Knowledge (SPCK), 1961. (Paper)

Burtt, Edwin A., ed. *The Teachings of the Compassionate Buddha.* (Mentor.) N.Y.: The New American Library of World Literature, Inc., 1955. (Paper)

Cooke, Gerald. *As Christians Face Rival Religions.* . . . N.Y.: Association Press, 1962.

Cragg, Kenneth. *The Call of the Minaret.* N.Y.: Oxford University Press, 1956.

Devanandan, Paul David. *The Concept of Māyā: An Essay . . . [on] the Hindu Theory of the World.* . . . London: Lutterworth Press, 1950.

Hamilton, Clarence Herbert, ed. *Buddhism, a Religion of Infinite Compassion: Selections from Buddhist Literature.* Indianapolis, Ind.: Liberal Arts Press, Inc., 1952. (Paper)

Hollis, Michael, bp. *Paternalism and the Church: A Study of South Indian Church History.* Toronto: Oxford University Press, 1962.

Ingham, Kenneth. *Reformers in India, 1793–1833; an Account of the Work of Christian Missionaries in Behalf of Social Reform.* London: Cambridge University Press, 1956.

Latourette, Kenneth Scott. *A History of Christianity.* 7 vols. N.Y.: Harper & Brothers, 1937–1945.

Morgan, Kenneth William, ed. *Islam the Straight Path: Islam Interpreted by Muslims.* N.Y.: The Ronald Press Co., 1958.

———. *Path of the Buddha: Buddhism Interpreted by Buddhists.* N.Y.: The Ronald Press Co., 1956.

———. *The Religion of the Hindus.* N.Y.: The Ronald Press Co., 1953.

Neill, Stephen Charles, bp. *Christian Faith and Other Faiths. . . .* N.Y.: Oxford University Press, 1961.

Newbigin, J. E. Leslie. *That All May Be One: A South India Diary.* (Haddon House Book.) N.Y.: Association Press, 1952.

Radhakrishnan, Sir Sarvepalli. *Eastern Religions and Western Thought.* (Galaxy Bk.) N.Y.: Oxford University Press, 1959. (Paper)

———. *The Hindu View of Life.* N.Y.: The Macmillan Co., 1962. (Paper)

Renou, Louis, ed. *Hinduism.* Englewood, N.J.: Prentice-Hall, Inc., 1962.

Schweitzer, Albert. *Indian Thought and Its Development.* Boston: Beacon Press, Inc., 1957. (Paper)

Selections from the Sacred Writings of the Sikhs. Translated by Trilochan Singh [and others]. (UNESCO Collection of Representative Works: India Series.) N.Y.: The Macmillan Co., 1960.

Singh, Khushwant. *The Sikhs.* London: George Allen & Unwin, Ld., 1953.

Smith, Wilfred Cantwell. *Islam in Modern History.* (Mentor.) N.Y.: The New American Library of World Literature, Inc., 1959. (Paper)

Tambimutta, Francis O. *A Profile of Ceylon's Catholic Heritage.* (World Horizon Reports, No. 28.) Maryknoll, N.Y.: Maryknoll Publications, [1961].

Zimmer, Heinrich Robert. *Philosophies of India*. N.Y.: Meridian Books, Inc., 1956. (Paper)

LITERATURE

The Bhagavad Gita. Translated by Juan Mascaró. Baltimore: Penguin Books, Inc., 1962. (Paper)

Bolitho, Hector. *Jinnah, Creator of Pakistan*. N.Y.: The Macmillan Co., 1955.

Brecher, Michael. *Nehru; a Political Biography*. N.Y.: Oxford University Press, 1959.

Fischer, Louis. *Gandhi: His Life and Message for the World*. (Signet Books.) The New American Library of World Literature, Inc., 1954. (Paper)

Fisher, Welthy Honsinger. *To Light a Candle*. N.Y.: McGraw-Hill Book Co., Inc., 1962. [Biography]

Gandhi, Mohandas Karamchand. *An Autobiography or the Story of My Experiments with Truth*. Boston: Beacon Press, Inc., 1957. (Paper)

———. *The Gandhi Reader; a Source Book of His Life and Writings*. Bloomington, Ind.; University of Indiana Press, 1956.

Gargi, Balwant. *Theatre in India*. N.Y.: Theatre Arts Books, 1962.

Graham, Carol. *Azariah of Dornakal*. Toronto: Macmillan Co. of Canada, Ltd., 1946. [Biography]

Kabir, Humayun, ed. *Green and Gold: Stories and Poems from Bengal*. Norfolk, Conn.: New Directions, 1958.

Kripalani, Krishna, ed. *All Men Are Brothers. The Life and Thoughts of Mahatma Gandhi as Told in His Own Words*. London: Longmans Green & Co., Ltd. (Orient Longmans), 1959.

READING LIST

Markandaya, Kamala. *Nectar in a Sieve*. (Signet Books.) N.Y.: The New American Library of World Literature, Inc., 1956. (Paper) [Fiction]

Mehta, Ved Parkash. *Face to Face: An Autobiography*. Boston: Little, Brown & Co., 1957.

Moraes, Francis Robert (Frank). *Jawaharlal Nehru; a Biography*. N.Y.: The Macmillan Co., 1956.

Muhammad Iqbal, Sir. *Poems*. Translated from the Urdu by V. G. Kiernan. Hollywood-by-the-Sea, Fla.: Transatlantic Arts, Inc., 1955.

Narayan, R. K. *The Bachelor of Arts*. East Lansing, Mich.: Michigan Stage College Press, 1954. [Fiction]

Rama Rau, Santha (Mrs. Faubion Bowers). *Gifts of Passage*. Harper & Brothers, 1961. [Autobiography]

Sheean, Vincent. *Nehru: The Years of Power*. N.Y.: Random House, Inc., 1960.

Siddiqui, Ashraf and Lerch, Marilyn, eds. *Toontoony Pie, and Other Tales from Pakistan*. N.Y.: The World Publishing Company, 1961.

A Tagore Reader. Edited by Amiya Chakravarty. (UNESCO Collection of Representative Works: India Series.) N.Y.: The Macmillan Co., 1961.

Tennyson, Hallam. *India's Walking Saint: The Story of Vinoba Bhave*. N.Y.: Doubleday & Co., Inc., 1955.

Thapar, Romila. *Indian Tales*. Toronto: Clarke, Irwin & Company, Ltd., [n.d.].

Vaid, Krishna B. *Steps in Darkness*. Translated from the Hindi. N.Y.: Orion Press, Inc., 1962. [Fiction]

Wilson, Dorothy Clarke. *Take My Hands: The Remarkable Story of Dr. Mary Verghese*. N.Y.: McGraw-Hill Book Co., Inc., 1963.

READING LIST

GENERAL

Abrecht, Paul. *The Churches and Rapid Social Change*. N.Y.: Doubleday & Co., Inc., 1961.

Faris, Donald K. *To Plow with Hope*. N.Y.: Harper & Brothers, 1958.

Foster, George McClelland. *Traditional Cultures and the Impact of Technological Change*. N.Y.: Harper & Brothers, 1962.

Kahin, George McTurnan, ed. *Major Governments of Asia*. Ithaca, N.Y.: Cornell University Press, 1958.

Vries, Egbert de. *Man in Rapid Social Change*. N.Y.: Doubleday & Co., Inc., 1961.

·

A WORD ABOUT THE FORMAT

The text of this book is set in Monotype Baskerville No. 353, 11 point leaded 2 points. This font, an exact reproduction of a roman letter first produced in England about 1757 by John Baskerville, the greatest printer and type founder of his time. His specimen of which are treated on the index of Caston, one of our planes, beauty, and a little printed by him in 1763 is to this date considered one of the finest examples of fine bookmaking art.

COMPOSED, PRINTED, AND BOUND BY THE PLIMPTON PRESS
NORWOOD, MASSACHUSETTS
PAPER BY ANTILLSON LOCATION, BRET, NEW YORK
HALF PAGES B. LA WARREN & SON COMPANY
TYPOGRAPHICAL DESIGN BY MARGARET W. SMITH

A WORD ABOUT THE FORMAT

The text of this book is set in Monotype Baskerville No. 353, 11 point leaded 3 points. This font is an exact reproduction of a roman letter first produced in England about 1757 by John Baskerville, the greatest printer and type founder of his time. His types, most of which are based on the letters of Caslon, are of exceptional beauty, and a Bible printed by him in 1763 is to this date considered one of the finest examples of the Bible-printing art.

COMPOSED, PRINTED, AND BOUND BY THE PLIMPTON PRESS, NORWOOD, MASSACHUSETTS
COVERS BY AFFILIATED LITHOGRAPHERS, INC., NEW YORK
TEXT PAPER: S. D. WARREN'S #66 ANTIQUE
TYPOGRAPHICAL DESIGN BY MARGERY W. SMITH

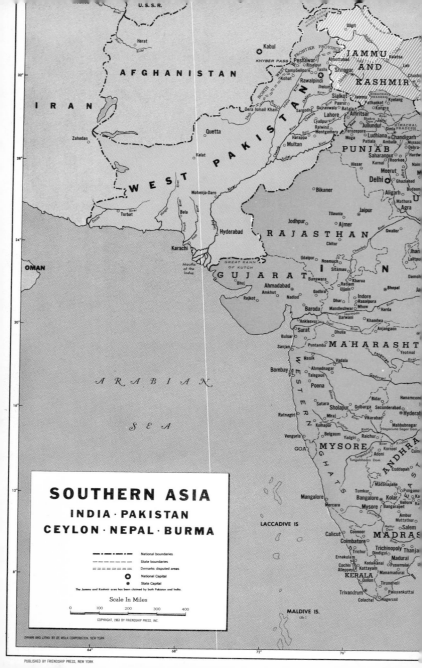

SOUTHERN ASIA

INDIA · PAKISTAN
CEYLON · NEPAL · BURMA

·—·—·—·	National boundaries
---------	State boundaries
=========	Demarks disputed areas
✪	National Capital
●	State Capital

The Jammu and Kashmir area has been claimed by both Pakistan and India.

Scale In Miles

0   100   200   300   400

COPYRIGHT, 1963 BY FRIENDSHIP PRESS, INC.

DRAWN AND LITHO. BY DE MOLA CORPORATION, NEW YORK

PUBLISHED BY FRIENDSHIP PRESS, NEW YORK

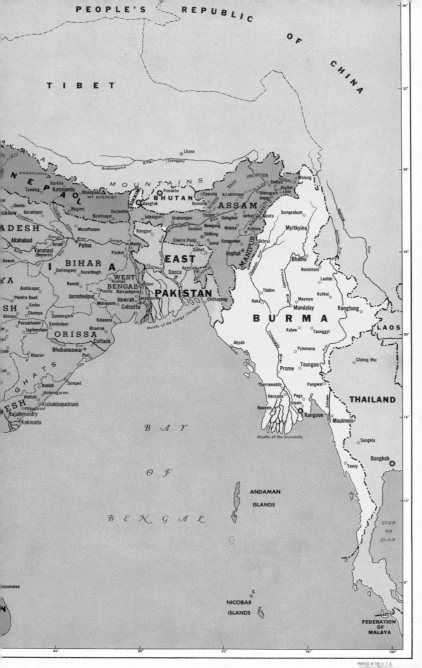